I0069251

Be Legendary

The Presence of Leadership: Strength and Vision

Sherri K. Baldwin
and
Rick M. Vipperman

Be Legendary: The Presence of Leadership: Strength and Vision

By Sherri K. Baldwin and Rick M. Vipperman

© 2018 Sherri K. Baldwin and Rick M. Vipperman
Printed in the United States of America

ISBN: 978-1-7320069-1-1
Library of Congress Control Number: 2018965642

All rights reserved solely by the author. The author guarantees all contents are original and do not infringe upon the legal rights of any other person or work. No part of this book may be reproduced, stored in a retrieval system, or transmitted in any form or by any means without expressed written permission of the author.

Published by Pearhouse Press, Pittsburgh, PA
PearhousePress.com

Author website: LeadAdvantageInc.com

Edited by Jessica Olma, Castle Rock, Co ScribeSyndicate.com

Cover Illustration by Taylor Cashdan TaylorCashdan.com

Photo credit: Prince David, Unsplash All rights reserved.

Table of Contents

More often than not, we lack a complete picture or full knowledge about a problem or situation. Regardless of the field we are in, discovery always begins with the search. Tapping into the collective wisdom of the team leads to anticipating and mitigating risks in addition to proactively seeking creative solutions to unexpected events.

Leaders understand that if we are going to be successful at anything we do—as an organization or as a team—we must have one critical and fundamental element in place at all times; a unity of purpose we also refer to as "The Why." It answers the question about why we do what we do. It is larger than an individual thought or goal and focuses on the greater good rather than our own self-interest.

Empowerment is either invaluable to an organization or valueless. It is also the most misunderstood, over-used and misused phrase by *managers*. However, *leaders* know that the source of their profitability and success is directly linked to the dynamic of empowerment.

People and numbers can be deceptive and misleading, but patterns of behavior always reveal the truth. These patterns are tied directly to how we think and act. This chapter begins with two of seven behavior patterns that reveal the opposing extremes in a person's view of the world.

Al Capone said, "*The only way three people can keep a secret is if two of them are dead.*" We demonstrate the reasoning behind this view as we explain three patterns in this chapter including "The Boss" who requires loyalty, the flamboyant character that draws attention with their grandiose ideas, and the meticulous and analytical bookkeeper with knowledge of every detail. Certain behaviors are associated with success and some are not.
The magic is in the mix.

There are no medals for trying. Strength comes from commitment and commitment is about "doing." This pattern sets a higher standard of commitment to success between leaders and the individuals or teams around them. Leaders are performance and achievement driven with uncompromising principles and values. This is the leader that people will follow into the Abyss.

A Chinese term *Wei Chi* is interpreted as "where danger meets opportunity." Any risk is a potential danger/obstacle or a potential opportunity. The people who are willing to take appropriate risks with new and different ideas are the leaders who advance our companies to the next level. The true enemy is settling for the status quo.

We do not deliberately set out to undermine our own success. It is usually an unintentional consequence of our actions or inactions that undermine our objective. To avoid these unintended consequences, leaders intentionally focus on specific measures that accomplish the desired results.

Acknowledgments

As we look back over our collective 50+ years of working in this leadership arena, there are many companies and individuals who have played an invaluable role in our success. It's only appropriate to acknowledge them and thank them for all of their support and confidence they have had in us throughout the years.

First and foremost, thank you to our spouses, George and Ann. Thank you for your patient tolerance of our travel through the years and meals on your own. Thank you for believing in us and what we are doing. Thank you for your encouragement and unselfish understanding as we continue to embrace our dream and something that we both love and have dedicated our careers to - impacting lives and making a difference in the careers of others.

Second, Bob Mobley, we express our gratitude to our Director of Learning and Analytics, who has been a colleague and friend for many years. Bob has made a significant contribution to the company and has faithfully supported us and our work through both challenging and exciting times.

Finally, we would like to acknowledge our "honor roll" of clients and individuals who have distinguished themselves within their industries and communities with their unique commitment to leadership development. Although this list is not all-inclusive, these companies represent many organizations we have worked with through the years and have a special place in our hearts:

- ***David Doctor, E4 Carolinas, a trade association for the energy industry in North and South Carolina.*** You have remained one of our biggest fans through the years and have allowed us to continue to work within the energy industry in the Carolinas and beyond. You are an inspiration to us and our work through your example of exceptional leadership. Also, thank you to Kelly Perkins who has gone above and beyond for us.

- **_Bruce Williams, National Gypsum_**. Thank you for almost 20 years of trust and partnership while developing all levels of your leadership teams. We appreciate the valuable friendship that has emerged over many years of working together.

- **_Joann Spaletta & Julie Cooper, Carolinas Healthcare, Area Health Education Center_**. You were our first clients with LeadAdvantage who were willing to take a risk and allow us the opportunity to demonstrate our process and its impact.

- **_Kelly Jordan, Coca-Cola Bottling Co_**. We appreciate your continued support and commitment to your company's leadership development. You challenged us to continue to develop customized programs for Coca-Cola throughout the years, and after three tiers of development, you asked for a fourth!

- **_Bill Perotti, Sylvia Dugosh and Rennae Flemming, Frost Bank in Texas_**. Thank you for all the fun and memories of working with you and your mid- to senior-level managers for over a decade.

- **_Scott Carlberg, The Carolinas Nuclear Cluster_**. Thank you for allowing us to "interview" with you by asking us to give a speech to 300 people before bringing us in to develop and deliver a process to Leadership Energy Carolinas.

- **_Jim Little, Industry Representative for the State of South Carolina's Governors Nuclear Advisory Board and Consultant_**. Thank you for all the morning coffee talks and continued interest in our work and leadership development in the industry.

- **_Chris Reen, The Oklahoman Media Company_**. We appreciate your support and allowing Jeanne Neugebauer and Scott Briggs to welcome us as part of your internal leadership development.

- **_ACE Hardware_**. We enjoyed being part of your development process for many years and allowing us to "knock your socks off."

- **_Walmart Stores_**. Thank you for making us an integral part of the leadership training process for over 15 years, holding over

20 programs a year for over 600 managers and supervisors each year, in both the US and internationally.

- *American Airlines*. Your chief pilot brought us in to encourage leadership qualities with all the pilots, most of whom had little or no leadership development other than technical courses. Thank you for understanding that balancing leadership and management is crucial to success.

- *More valuable contributors to our success*: IBM, Robert Morris Banking Association, Husqvarna, Belk Store Services, JC Penney, Microsoft, Chiron America, University of South Carolina, K-Line Trucking Company, United States Gypsum Co, The Container Corporation, Comporium Communications Corporation, Handleman Corporation, Norwest Bank (currently Wells Fargo), Banco Popular in Puerto Rico, Charlotte Observer, Duke Energy, Siemens Energy, and the United States Coast Guard.

Introduction

Leadership Is the Most Powerful Force Known to Organizations

"It is essential for leaders to integrate their hearts with their heads by developing self-awareness and emotional intelligence while empowering people to do the same."[1]
– Bill George, Professor of Management Practices at Harvard Business School and former Chair of Medtronic, Inc.

We believe our job, regardless of what position in the organization, is ultimately to make the company money, and it is how we get there that separates and defines authentic leaders. In the quote above, Bill George was speaking about authentic leadership.

Let's establish clearly: *We believe when used correctly, leadership is the most powerful force we possess.*

In this context, **leadership** is a rarity. We know it when we see it, and we know when we don't. In a roomful of people, if there is a leader present, they are easy to find. That leader may or may not speak, but their presence will simply capture your attention. Like a great piece of art that draws us into the painting, we are captivated by that leader.

---

[1] http://www.billgeorge.org/page/an-important-new-book-conscious-capitalism-by-john-mackey

Visible Leadership – Rick

For example, you might prefer using your time to think, reflect, and relax as I do when flying on an airplane. I was nearing the end of my four-year obligation in the Air Force and flying to Charlotte, NC on a 10-day leave to pursue potential future career opportunities. The furthest thing from my mind was engaging in the typical, *"what do you do?"* dialogue with a stranger. I often put on my headset, read a book, look out the window or close my eyes, and communicate through nonverbal signals that I prefer not to engage in a long conversation. However, on this particular flight, as a large number of people were boarding, putting their luggage in the overhead compartments, and looking for their seats, I noticed a passenger already in the seat next to mine. Given my preference for not wanting to engage in flight conversations, I was surprised at how quickly we established a rapport, and I was certainly impressed with his demeanor, style, and presence. He was inquisitive, quick-witted and genuine.

We continued to have a very relaxed and natural discussion for the entire flight. It was more than halfway through the flight before he mentioned that he was Executive Vice President of Human Resources for NCNB, currently Bank of America. The flight went by very quickly and as the plane landed, he handed me his card and said, *"When you have a chance, give me a call. I would like to continue our conversation."*

I took him up on his invitation and never anticipated he would offer me a job with the bank before my leave ended. To my great surprise, he did. Those leadership qualities that I noticed when I got on that flight continued to be revealed and evident to me throughout my six years at NCNB. I ended up moving into leadership development with the bank, which became my life-long passion and career.

Meet the Authors

Rick and Sherri, co-authors of this book, have a combined fifty years of experience in leadership development, leadership behavior research and consulting with many leading companies, some of which are the most successful organizations in the world; Walmart, IBM, Ace Hardware, American Airlines, and Coca-Cola Bottling Company, among others.

Throughout this book, we have included examples from many of these companies, and input or comments from many of the session participants from our leadership programs and consulting. Traditionally, many organizations cut leadership development programs during challenging times. However, most of the companies listed above realize that it is even more important to increase leadership development, to focus and refine the qualities known to move their companies forward through tough economic periods. All these organizations, regardless of the industry, have one understanding in common: *the necessity of continuing to develop and strengthen the leadership qualities of their management teams*, not only to navigate tumultuous times but to accomplish the objective of taking their companies efficiently and effectively to a higher plateau. As one executive expressed to us, *"Why would any organization choose to face any situation, particularly a downturn in the economy, with unprepared and underdeveloped employees and expect to succeed. Failure to make that investment a priority would be a great risk to the company. To think otherwise is simply false economy."*

**Leadership will always make the difference.
That is why we do what we do and
that is what our work is all about.**

*This book will empower you to add value with
your presence and to create and foster
leadership at every level in your organization.*

To work, to think, to take away something real...

Services:

Group and Individual High-Potential and Senior Level Coaching

Creating a Sustainable and Performance-Driven Team
and Organizational Culture

Mid to Senior Level Leadership Development

High-Potential and Mentoring programs

*le ad*vantage
developing your team

www.leadadvantageinc.com

Prepared

The pilot, Captain "Sully" Sullenberger, who safely landed his US Airways flight in the Hudson River, continually emphasized in his account of the incident how **preparation was tantamount to the right execution by a leader.**

> *"The bonds among pilots were paramount. At each base where I was stationed, we were reminded again and again how vital it was to know about the dangers of complacency, to have as much knowledge as possible about the particular plane you were flying, to be aware of every aspect of what you were doing. Being a fighter pilot involved risk—we all knew that—and some accidents happened owing to circumstances beyond a pilot's control. But with diligence, **preparation**, judgment, and skill, you could minimize your risks. And we needed one another to do that."* [2]

> *"America labeled Charles Lindbergh as 'Lucky Lindy,' but he knew better. We read his 1927 book about his famous transatlantic trip. In it, he made clear that his success was due almost entirely to preparation, not luck, or as I prefer to call it, circumstance. The nickname, 'Prepared Lindy' may not have had the same magical ring to it, but his views of pilot **preparation** have long resonated with me ... flights are almost always routine, but every time we push back from the gate, we must be **prepared** for the unexpected."* [3]

---

[2] C. Sullenberger and J. Zaslow, 2009. Highest Duty: My Search for What Really Matters

[3] C. Sullenberger and J. Zaslow, 2009. Highest Duty: My Search for What Really Matters

Fighter pilot Lt. Heather Penney was also given a similar nickname, "Lucky Penney." During the events of September 11, 2001 (9/11), Penney was given her orders to take down United Airlines flight 93 that was heading toward Washington, and most likely, the White House.[4]

> *"The one thing she didn't have as she roared into the crystalline sky was live ammunition. Or missiles. Or anything at all to throw at a hostile aircraft. Except her own plane. So that was the plan...She muttered a fighter pilot's prayer — 'God, don't let me [expletive] up.'"* - **The Washington Post**.[5]

There was something larger than life at stake and she was **prepared** to do whatever it took to handle the unexpected. Similarly, leaders are **prepared** for the unexpected.

---

[4]   S. Hendrix, Washington Post, 2011. F-16 pilot was ready to give her life on Sept. 11

[5]   S. Hendrix, Washington Post, 2011. F-16 pilot was ready to give her life on Sept. 11

CHAPTER 1

Tapping the Unknown

Pilots spend most of their flight training **preparing** for what can go wrong. They continually ask:

- What are the various obstacles that pose the greatest risk?
- How can I mitigate those risks?

Attorneys prepare for trial by anticipating the questions from the opposing side and preparing a strategy to overcome any damaging line of questioning.

In that same way, leaders **prepare** to mitigate problems by going through various "what if" scenarios with their team. Leaders cannot afford to be absent or unengaged. They must be present, purposely focused and prepared for any challenge. Through extensive due diligence, leaders prepare for the challenges and dangers that can get in the way of their success, or worse, create the "knock-out punch" in the implementation of their plans, projects, and tasks. Leaders approach these issues by addressing something that we refer to as, "tapping the unknown."

Donald Rumsfeld, Secretary of Defense under George W. Bush, referred to this phenomenon in his book, *The Known and the Unknowns*. Secretary Rumsfeld wrote,

"There are known knowns, known unknowns,
and unknown unknowns."

He defines the **"known knowns"** as "anything we have knowledge of such as gravity, where we know something will eventually fall from the sky. The **'known unknowns'** are described as gaps in our knowledge, but they are gaps we know exist. We know for example, that the exact extent of Iran's nuclear weapons program is unknown to us. If we ask the right questions, we can potentially fill those gaps in our knowledge. Eventually making what is unknown a 'known known.'

"The category of 'unknown unknowns' is the most difficult to grasp. They are gaps in our knowledge but gaps we do not know exist. Genuine surprises tend to arise out of this category. Nineteen hijackers using commercial airliners as guided missiles to incinerate 3,000 men, women and children was perhaps the single most horrific **'unknown unknown'** America has experienced."

Leaders tap into the unknowns by factoring the potential obstacles into the planning process to be prepared for any future event. By going through this exercise, the message to the team is to remove many of the obstacles up front. Secondly, we can be in "ready mode" by having contingency plans for the other, less controllable events. However, leaders also realize that despite going through these scenarios, a "what the hell just happened" event may sometimes still occur. One that no one could have predicted.

Encountering an Unknown:
Focus on What Matters Most! - *Sherri*

I remember one of those "unknown" moments in life. I pursued my pilot's license several years back. Most of the training I received was preparing me for what can go wrong or get in the way of reaching my destination. For those of you who have been in a small two- or four-seat aircraft, Cessna, Piper Tomahawk, you will relate to how small those planes actually are inside. There are two seats up front with the pilot seat on the left and the door rubbing against the pilot's left leg. The passenger is on the right with one leg touching the pilot and the other touching the right door. These planes are not made for comfort or for those who are claustrophobic.

Now, I am not claustrophobic, however, I am afraid of heights. So, you may be asking, "What the hell are you doing flying a plane?" Not to worry. I am not nervous on a plane because I am closed in with windows and doors; it's situations like standing on the edge of a cliff in the open air that makes me feel dizzy.

When everything is going smoothly, a plane almost flies itself. Flight training is mostly for anticipating and being…
prepared for the unexpected.

I had prepared through my training to overcome obstacles such as losing power or instrument failure, ways to land in a field if necessary, losing radio contact, bad weather, and how to make appropriate adjustments along the flight path to keep on course and land safely. But, I had not prepared for my door flying open during take-off. Yikes! Finding myself unexpectedly looking straight down 1,000 feet to the ground, my door no longer touching my left leg, panic and fear tried to overtake me. I temporarily had no idea what to do next.

Then I remembered what my flight instructor always said, "*Sherri, fly the plane first or nothing else matters.*" That helped me to focus on what mattered most…**flying the plane**. I immediately looked out the window to avoid other possible threats such as hitting a flock of birds or another plane. Then I was able to look at my map, talk on the radio, and close my door - which all seemed important and/or urgent at the time - but came second to flying the plane.

Do What You Were Hired to Do

I share this story because the advice is perfect for business as well. When clutter – such as paperwork, meetings, emails, phone calls, etc. – start piling up and getting in the way of what is important, remember to focus on what matters most.

Do what you were hired to do, or nothing else matters.

In other words, if you are not focusing on completing your job, you can lose perspective on priorities, and confuse the clutter with actions that are necessary for you to do your job.

Casey Stengel was an American Major League Baseball player. His career also included managing the New York Yankees, the New York Mets, the Atlanta Braves, and the LA Dodgers. He was elected to the Baseball Hall of Fame in 1966. Stengel would often say, "The main thing is to keep the main thing, the main thing."

At times, we may find ourselves so caught up in busy work that it begins to consume our time, focus and attention. It is an allusion that robs us of our productivity and eventually we think of this clutter as our job. We might call it substitute activity. Busy work may simply be substituting what's immediate for what's important and necessary.

> **Your job is defined as:** *the one thing you must accomplish every day before you turn off the lights and go home in order for the team, department, division or company to be more successful.*

Meetings, telephone calls, and emails are all secondary clutter getting in the way of the real job at hand. We must "focus on what matters" and "keep the main thing, the main thing."

Recently, we were asked by one of our clients to consult with a Vice President of the company about his job and how he was prioritizing his days. This came about because he was in charge of several different areas of the company and his manager was concerned with how he was balancing the various responsibilities and his lack of timely responsiveness. To help with the initial prioritizing, we had him complete a pie chart dividing how he spent his time on any given day or week. The chart is based on a drawing by that client. As you can see, he divided his pie into five areas of responsibility showing 65% of his time spent in internal or external meetings.

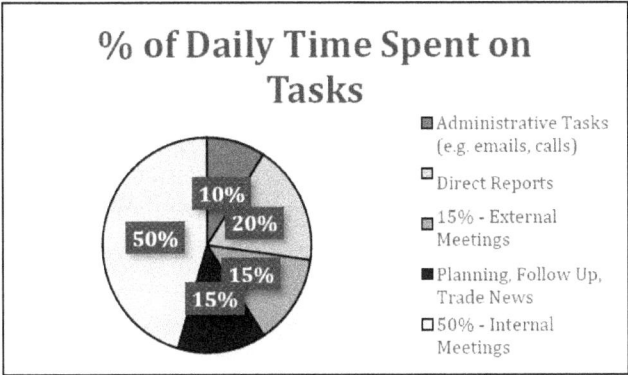

% of Daily Time Spent on Tasks

- Administrative Tasks (e.g. emails, calls)
- Direct Reports
- 15% - External Meetings
- Planning, Follow Up, Trade News
- 50% - Internal Meetings

This is a Vice President who is supposed to be focused on several energy-related areas in his company.

Looking at the pie, what would you determine his main job to be within the company? It clearly has become focusing on clutter.

The pie chart **totals 110%.** He had lost awareness of time and how to manage it effectively and had to stretch it by working overtime to make up for the loss in other quality-focused areas.

Ask yourself:
- What would your chart reveal about you and your job?

If you divide your job responsibilities between where you are spending most of your time compared with where you should be spending your time, often there is a measurable gap or discrepancy. What is the one thing that you must do to be successful? That answer is priority number one.

As leaders, we need to determine if the time spent on each responsibility is proportionate to our priorities, realizing that "clutter" can become a larger piece of the pie if we are not careful.

To illustrate this point, one of the major Minneapolis based banking clients we have worked with decided to test this principle after their executive team went through our leadership process, including the exercise we described above. Six months later we received an email from the president of the company. The letter explained that the executive team decided to take two individuals from their marketing and business development division to learn what would happen if they actually spent 90 percent of their time on their job, selling the bank's products and services.

After arranging to have their non-sales duties covered for a period of two months, the results of that endeavor, from the president, are on the following page.

Results of Time/Task Management Study

Productive Activities	Increase from April to May	Increase from May to June
Sales Calls	44%	165%
Referrals Made	17%	214%
Referrals Closed	30%	171%
Bank Deposits	45%	55%
Team Morale	Definitely Increased!!	

Two individuals, Sue and Wendy, made 171% improvement in their performance in only two months which resulted in a bottom line improvement in bank deposits of 55%. What if you added a third person or a 10th or a 20th…it is difficult to imagine an increase of that magnitude!

We have good news and bad news. The bad news is we will never completely get rid of clutter and be able to focus 90 or 100 % of our time on our number one priority. Like waves on a beach continually returning so does clutter. The reality is we must attend certain meetings and respond to emails and sometimes focus on "other" responsibilities. It becomes necessary to constantly refocus and redirect.

The good news is, if we could find just 5 or 10% more time to focus on our number one priority, it would make a significant improvement in our job. Leaders look for paths to improvement not only for themselves but also for their teams. Think about the aggregate of those numbers and what a tremendous impact that would have on your bottom line!

Your competitors are also looking for that extra 5 to 10 %, and whoever gets there first wins a major competitive advantage. Every day we pick up the paper and we read about those who make their way to the winners' circle and those who are no longer around to compete. Leaders understand how to prioritize and discern what is really important versus what is perceived to be urgent or vital for the moment.

We took away some key nuggets about managing clutter adopted from *Leading an Inspired Life* by Jim Rohn:

"Some will master, and some will serve." The nature of life is to make sure *you* become the master. You have to run the day, or it will run you. **You must stay in charge.**

You probably know some people around you who are just plain busy being busy. **You've got to be busy being productive.** Don't mistake movement for achievement.

Unity

Louis V. Gerstner, Jr., the chairman and CEO of IBM from April 1993 until March 2002, led IBM from the brink of bankruptcy back into the forefront of the technology business. Lou Gerstner said in his book, *Who Says Elephants Can't Dance?*

> *"Until I came to IBM, I probably would have told you that culture was just one among several important elements in any organization's makeup and success—along with vision, strategy, marketing, financials, and the like. I came to see, in my time at IBM, that (team) culture isn't just one aspect of the game; it is the game. In the end, an organization (or team) is nothing more than the collective capacity of its people to create value."[6]*

---

[6]   D. Elenberg, 2003. Developer Works, Index San Francisco, Book review -- Who Says Elephants Can't Dance?

CHAPTER 2

The Why

In chapter one, we looked at removing clutter and focusing on what matters. We can't think with clarity until we remove the confusion of clutter. Once we have done that, we can be intentional about creating sustainable success for our team and organization. The only way to create what Lou Gerstner is talking about is to be unified and united around a common cause, what we call a "unity of purpose."

As we were thinking about writing this book and collaborating about our experiences in the leadership arena, we knew we had to start with what matters most to leaders—having a "unity of purpose."

How would you define Unity of Purpose?

When we ask this question in our leadership sessions, we frequently hear that unity of purpose is some version of a mission statement. However, this is a myth that needs to be clarified.

A mission statement is NOT a Unity of Purpose.

- Why do firemen willingly run into burning buildings?
- Why is the Secret Service willing to take a bullet for the president?
- Why do soldiers "leave no man behind"?
- What is it that unites and unifies individuals to support a cause to the extent that they are willing to risk and potentially sacrifice themselves for a higher purpose?

"Unity of purpose" energizes a team to think and operate as one unit fighting for the same cause. Our job at LeadAdvantage is to un-complicate or simplify the "unity of purpose." We believe it is "The Why." The reason we do what we do. It is why we are sometimes willing to work 45-50 plus hours a week, come into the office over the weekend, or postpone vacations to complete a project. It is why we are willing to occasionally miss our child's soccer match or dinner with the family, arriving home late after the kids are already in bed.

**Unity of purpose is why we are willing to
make personal sacrifices to be part of
something we believe in; something special.**

This Above All, by Erik Knight, really captured this point for us. The author tells a story about the Battle of Dunkirk, a devastating defeat for England that later became a defining moment. This battle took place in Dunkirk, France, during the Second World War between the Allies and Germany. The war had dragged on and on and the morale was at an all-time low.

Following the devastating defeat at Dunkirk, morale sank even lower. This is the point where the book picks up with a veteran soldier and a young lieutenant reflecting on what happened; this is the essence of their conversation:

> The young lieutenant said, *"I don't understand what went wrong. In the military, we are taught to fight with organization, discipline, and unity. But what you are saying to me is in the Battle of Dunkirk, there was no organization, discipline, and unity. "*

> The veteran soldier replied, *"You are right, son. We are taught to fight with organization and discipline, but at Dunkirk, the chain of command failed the soldiers by not reminding them of what we were fighting and sacrificing for - our purpose."*

Without being reminded of the purpose and "The Why," the soldiers were laying down their arms and walking off the battlefield, hence, the devastating defeat.

Understanding Purpose

If we understand our purpose and what we are fighting for, "The Why" generates the will to fight to the bitter end for our cause. If we do not know "The Why," we do not understand our purpose, or no longer remember what we are fighting for, then we will lay down our arms and walk off your battlefield. We will either figuratively, mentally, or literally check out.

⚘

**Unity of Purpose is creating something
everyone believes in that unites a team.**

⚘

**How do you know that you have created that type of unified
purpose on your team?**

Your team visibly demonstrates a willingness to share
individually and collectively, their time, energy and effort to
achieve higher standards and greater outcomes.
That spirit of willingness is legendary.

Following the Battle of Dunkirk, British Prime Minister Winston Churchill, reunited and rallied the nation by reminding his countrymen of what they were fighting for with one of his most famous speeches, *We Shall Fight on the Beaches*. It ends with,

> *"We shall go on to the end, we shall fight in
> France, we shall fight on the seas and oceans, we
> shall fight with growing confidence and growing
> strength in the air, we shall defend our Island,*

*whatever the cost may be, we shall fight on the
beaches, we shall fight on the landing grounds, we
shall fight in the fields and in the streets, we shall
fight in the hills; we shall never surrender..."*[7]

Churchill inspired his nation to have the courage and spirit to fight and never give up

What completes the unity is helping your team see what you as the leader envision. They need to be able to put themselves in the verbally painted picture that you create. Your team can then actually begin to visualize victory.

∽

Aristotle said, "*The 'soul' never thinks without a picture.*"

∽

For example, Martin Luther King's, *I Have a Dream,* speech united people in a peaceful manner by giving them a vision. His words empowered them to act on that vision by appropriately standing up for what is right and making the decision to treat all people in an equal manner. He helped others see how they could work toward equality. That is empowering the vision. He did not call for confrontation or riots in the street but motivated them to act by standing up for and believing in something greater than themselves.

Ronald Reagan gave an empowering speech and a visual that people will never forget with his *Shining City on a Hill Farewell Address,*

---

[7] © Chartwell Trust. Reprinted by permission Curtis Brown, London, The International Churchhill Society, https://www.winstonchurchill.org/resources/speeches/1940-the-finest-hour/we-shall-fight-on-the-beaches

"I've spoken of the shining city all my political life, but I don't know if I ever quite communicated what I saw when I said it. But in my mind, it was a tall, proud city built on rocks stronger than oceans, windswept, God-blessed, and teeming with people of all kinds living in harmony and peace; a city with free ports that hummed with commerce and creativity. And if there had to be city walls, the walls had doors and the doors were open to anyone with the will and the heart to get here. That's how I saw it and see it still."

Think about Lucky Penney from the first chapter. Two planes had already flown into the Twin Towers in New York City - the symbol of our greatness. One plane had flown into the Pentagon, and a second, United Flight 93, was assumed to be targeting the White House. Penney never had to make the ultimate sacrifice because Todd Beamer and the passengers on flight 93 made that decision before it became necessary. They tried to take back control of the plane, which ultimately crashed into a field in Pennsylvania, avoiding a horrific attack on our nation's capital.

Penney was willing to sacrifice her life for a cause she believed was greater than the life of any single individual, and Todd Beamer was able to unify and empower a plane full of passengers with two words, *"Let's Roll."*

꒰

We do not define Unity of Purpose.
Unity of purpose defines us; who we are and what we are.

꒰

"One life is all we have, and we live it as we believe in living it. But to sacrifice what you are and to live without belief, that is a fate more terrible than dying." - **Jeanne d'Arc**

The Locker Room

For most of us, our leadership will not be defined by a single event or action. That's probably a good thing because most of those moments are preceded by a catastrophic event where someone is catapulted into becoming legendary because of the action they take that literally elevates that person to such a status like Todd Beamer during 9/11. For most of us though, our leadership will be defined by a series of continuous smaller steps we take throughout our career that ultimately define us as a leader or a legendary leader.

Herb Kelleher, founder and former president and CEO of Southwest Airlines, created and empowered a vision that has led to over 45 years of consecutive profitable winning seasons. In the airline industry where most airlines have continuously lost money, Kelleher's unifying motto was: **Freedom to Fly and Democratize the Skies**. He wanted to create a fun, affordable, and accessible airline. It was the constant small things he did that combined to make such a big impact. He met customers, personally talked with employees, brought in snacks, and had fun over the years. Largely because of his pioneering efforts in the aviation industry, passenger travel increased from only 15 % of the population flying in the early 70's to 85 % in the mid-80's.[8]

Bryant Gumbel, an American television journalist, and sportscaster, had a number of NFL players on his show, HBO Real Sports, who left the game because of injuries or retirement. He was talking with them about what they missed most about the sport. Gumbel expected them to say the fans, the glory, breaking records, or being a celebrity, but unexpectedly, none of them mentioned any of those things. They all unanimously said what they missed most was the locker room. Bryant asked what it was about the locker room that made them miss it the most. Their responses included:

---

[8]   Blackwell, Charles W. "Flying High with Herb Kelleher: A Profile in Charismatic Leadership," *Journal of Leadership Studies*, June 22, 1999.

■ Genuine concern for one another ■ Trust ■ Hold one another accountable ■ The "work hard and play hard" mindset ■ Positive attitude ■ No whining rule	■ Team-above-self ethic ■ Sense of family ■ Having one another's back ■ Self-sacrifice ■ Learning from failure, by studying films ■ Celebrating success together

Essentially, Herb Kelleher created that locker room environment at Southwest Airlines. A certain Stanford University Graduate School of Business class consisting of corporate executives were skeptical that a company could create such an environment. After reading about Southwest Airlines in a case study, the executives visited the Airline to study the organization and interview employees as a class project. Kevin McNamara, Director of Worldwide Training for Burger King said,

> *"While I first thought no company can be as good as the case described, I found that the case didn't exaggerate at all, and in fact, may not have completely captured how well Southwest Airlines does treat its employees and customers."*

When the Stanford graduate students asked Southwest employees what made Southwest so different, their responses were similar to the sports players above:

▪ Friendly attitude ▪ Team above self ▪ Genuine concern for one another ▪ Family-oriented ▪ Trust ▪ Hold one another accountable ▪ No whining rule ▪ Work hard-play hard mindset	▪ Enjoy and make work fun ▪ Use your common sense ▪ Challenge the rules if they get in the way ▪ Be supportive of one another ▪ Wear your enthusiasm to work

If Bryant Gumbel ever decides to have retired Southwest employees on his show and asks them what they missed most about Southwest, they would likely respond the same as the NFL players and attribute it to the "locker room" environment.

Employees see this environment, experience the atmosphere, notice the difference it makes, and the impact it has on morale and production. They want to imitate the unique experience at every level in the organization.

If you lose the locker room environment, you lose the team.

In terms of your own organization, the same is true. Allowing poor behavior to continue, allowing a lack of accountability or too much conflict will result in apathy, low morale, clock-in and clock-out mentality, and turnover. The same is true if a team member can continue to disrupt the "locker room" by instigating negative gossip, argument or a bad attitude. It will pull the entire team down like a virus that spreads and contaminates every member of the team, destroying its cohesiveness. Leaders will not tolerate this divisive behavior. They will offer every opportunity for a change in conduct but will step up and make a tough call if and when it is necessary.

Phil Jackson, perhaps the greatest coach in NBA history, coached the Chicago Bulls and won six NBA championships. He then went to the LA Lakers and won three in a row (five total), before becoming president of the New York Knicks. In his book, *Sacred Hoops*, he says his philosophy is key to building a successful team. Phil,

> *"calls on the player's need to connect with something larger than themselves. It requires the individuals involved to surrender their self-interest for the greater good so that the whole adds up to more than the sum of its parts."*

Doesn't that apply to the workplace as well?

Empowered

At Southwest, every employee was united around the vision and the purpose, and Kelleher **empowered** them to achieve that vision. He created leaders who created leadership at every level in the organization. One employee stated, *"We are empowered to make on-the-spot decisions. We have the latitude to take care of the problem. There is no need for approval."*

This is empowering individuals and teams and is a tangible way of transferring responsibility and authority to individuals.

CHAPTER 3

The Money Trail

The Payoff of Empowerment

The payoff to Southwest Airlines for creating this type of environment:

- Profitability for 45+ consecutive years
- Southwest stock at its height earned the highest returns of any publicly traded US stock - a compounded return of over 21,000 %. Only Walmart came close.[9]

Many **managers** are reluctant to empower their employees because of control-related issues. However, **leaders** understand there is a far greater benefit to empowerment than there is potential risk.

Have you ever had a situation where you were unhappy with a service you received? You question the nearest employee about the apparent problem and the conversation ended unpleasantly with you saying, "*Let me speak with your supervisor.*" On the other hand, if the conversation had ended with the employee saying, "*I will take care of it,*" obviously, your impression of that company would be completely different. That kind of empowerment leads to customer loyalty.

Empowerment

We hire based on certain skills, spend money training and developing individuals, but often those talents go untapped because **managers** are not willing to properly empower those employees. Empowerment is a commonly overused term. People

---

[9]   Article, Stanford Graduate School of Business, Professor Charles O'Reilly and Jeffrey Pfeffer

give it different meanings, misuse and abuse it. Too many people think of empowerment as simply delegating. That is only one part of the definition. So, let's define empowerment.

Empowerment includes giving someone the appropriate responsibility and clearly defined authority, noting any specific circumstances or exceptions where the individual must check with their manager before proceeding. Outside the defined exceptions, the individual has complete authority to make decisions and take action. However, the individual must also fully understand they are accepting accountability for the outcome whether celebrating a great success for wins, meeting an adequate outcome, or falling short of expectations.

I (Sherri) previously worked in a hotel as Director of Sales and Marketing. When I started with the hotel, I made an argument for advertising locally versus nationally. At the time, most hotels were gaining 80% of their business from out of state, whereas, Charlotte was receiving a majority of their business from companies situated locally. I felt most of our advertising dollars should remain local. The Divisional director said they hired me because I knew the market in Charlotte and that I could use my advertising budget as I deemed appropriate. I was empowered to make financial decisions regarding advertising as long as I stayed within the budget.

However, he also said that I would be held accountable for the hotel's level of profitability as a result of how I spent those dollars – I owned it.

As management, we can transfer responsibility, but we cannot transfer the full measure of accountability. **We, as the leader, remain ultimately accountable.** However, we've got to be sure a mechanism is in place where the empowered individual shares in the pleasure or the pain. All three components have to be present for it to be true empowerment: responsibility, defined authority and accountability. A breakdown typically occurs with failure to clearly define the authoritative role or when the empowered individual accepts responsibility but rejects being blamed or held accountable when something goes wrong.

A fitting example of accountability comes from one of our clients, David Doctor. In the late 1980s, David was a co-founder of an energy trading business, a company that would buy and resell energy products at a profit. At the time, energy trading was a relatively new business and mostly attracted young people to work in that field. At 37, David was the "old" guy in the business. He had young traders working for him who bought and resold natural gas. The New York Mercantile Exchange introduced a natural gas futures contract around the same time, compounding the complexity and initially increasing the risk of natural gas trading. The company was part employee-owned. This young team built it into a billion-dollar business.

One day the head trader came to David's office. The trader's face was ashen, and he looked extremely nervous. David had always encouraged his staff to tell him the bad news first, as the good news always seemed to take care of itself.

David also knew that fast action could often correct an issue. He assured his team there would not be negative consequences from him if the individual(s) were honest and upfront about any potential problems.

The head trader, still fearful of losing his job, said that his team had made a trade error and just lost the company one million dollars and there was no way to get it back. It was gone. David was thoughtful for a moment and then responded,

> *"The Company has just made a one-million-dollar tuition investment in you and your team. You're now one million dollars smarter and better than earlier today. So, go back to work and employ that."*

David kept his promise not to overreact with penalizing consequences to the bad news since the trader had followed David's principle and came to him up front and fully acknowledged ownership. The financial loss could have destroyed the company and 160 people could have been without a job. And what if the trader had not told David immediately and waited until the end of the month believing that he would be penalized or even fired?

- The surprise disclosure could have upset many financial arrangements upon which the company depended.
- The trader could have kept the secret or tried to blame someone or something else.

Thankfully, neither outcome occurred. Both individuals did the right thing and as a result, the company prospered.

∼

By the end of the month, the team had rallied and turned up the intensity, trading out investments to offset the one-million-dollar loss, and actually made a profit.

∼

As the leader, there are rare circumstances when empowerment should be taken back. For credibility reasons, only extenuating circumstances should cause that to happen, such as an ethical violation or a situation gone terribly wrong. In other words, in empowered organizations, when mishaps occur, a leader coaches and advises knowing that part of development is learning from mistakes. However, once it is beyond that point and hits crisis mode, the leader takes back control to avoid a potential knockout punch.

In David's case, the loss was potentially a knockout punch. The tendency for many **managers** would likely be to take back control and deal strongly with the individual. David's courage as a **leader**, even though the situation qualified as a crisis, still prevailed. He did not step back in and take control. He knew he had to trust the team to make it right. He did not know if they would be successful, but he knew he had to let it play out and live by his values, or he would have lost the trust of the entire team. As a result, the company ultimately prospered, and the team stayed intact.

An example of a lack of accountability and where management should have taken back control was recorded in a 2016 issue of the Charlotte Observer. The headlines read: *"Warren to CEO: 'You should resign.'"* The Deon Roberts article recapped the U.S. Senate Committee's hearing on one of the country's largest corporations. The employees had allegedly engaged in illegal sales practices. It resulted in 5,300 employees being fired from the company between 2011 and 2016 for fraud and falsifying records for performance goals.

The article noted that Democratic Massachusetts U.S. Senator Elizabeth Warren said, *"This is about accountability."* She accused the CEO at the time, of "gutless" management and told him he should resign.

Ms. Warren went on to say,

> *"You haven't returned a single nickel of your personal earnings. You haven't fired a single senior executive. Instead, evidently, your definition of accountable is to push the blame to your low-level employees who don't have the money for fancy PR firms to defend themselves."*

Warren began her questioning by citing the company's Vision and Values Statement, particularly its suggestion, *"If you want to find out how strong a company's ethics are, don't listen to what its people say, watch what they do."* The CEO ultimately did resign.

Elizabeth Warren was essentially saying that the company CEO did not *demonstrate* accountability and it became an ethical issue when he failed to act and take back control once he knew about the fraud.

Legendary Leaders always take responsibility for their action or lack of action before they get caught. Leaders will plead "mea culpa" when something goes wrong. This means leaders will own up to their mistakes, accept the consequences, and find a way to rectify the situation. However, they also expect the same response from those around them. They expect to hear, "I will take care of it." What they will **not tolerate** is blaming someone or something else. It is one of five tripwires we will discuss in upcoming chapters that will cause a leader to move quickly from a leadership role to a management role. In other words, the conversation will become increasingly more direct.

Not meanness, but you know they mean business.

Summation:

Empowerment is not delegating and disappearing. It is about the presence of leadership, which creates an atmosphere of unity, support, and encouragement. We need to remain close enough to support but far enough away where the empowered person can make decisions, take risks, be creative, solve problems, and own the accountability. When empowerment is delegated correctly, meaning all three elements are in place - responsibility, defined authority and accountability - the individual will take ownership and do whatever it takes to be successful. The power of self-determination, unconstrained free will, and commitment to accomplishment, become the driving forces of success.

Ultimately the Big 3: profitability, productivity and efficiency, are all tied into how well we can empower those around us.

Patterns of Behavior

"There are many qualities that make a great leader. But having strong beliefs, being able to stick with them through popular and unpopular times, is the most important characteristic of a great leader." - **Rudy Giuliani, former Mayor, New York City**[10]

Rudolph W. Giuliani likens himself to a boxer who never takes a punch without swinging back. As mayor of New York City, he made the vengeful roundhouse an instrument of government, clipping anyone who crossed him. He picked fights with a notable lack of discrimination. He challenged city and state comptrollers, a few corporations, and the odd council member. He is the only man to ever take on five of the most notorious mob families in New York; he broke every one of them and sent the head of each of those mafia families to prison. Mr. Giuliani retells his stories of childhood toughness, of standing up to bullies who mocked his love of opera and his Yankee loyalties.[11]

For Mayor Giuliani, what catapulted him from a strong manager to a great leader were the events following 9/11. He became known as "America's Mayor." The fighting spirit he grew up with helped him stand strong during a catastrophic event. He remained calm and addressed the American people with composure and determination in the midst of utter chaos, confusion, burning buildings, and unparalleled nationwide fear. As a result, Giuliani was able to transfer that calmness to the American people through a message that united and helped everyone believe we would

---

[10] Brainy Quote, https://www.brainyquote.com/quotes/quotes/r/rudygiulia173443.html

[11] New York Times article, 2008. M. Powell and R. Buettner, 2008. In Matters Big and Small, Crossing Giuliani Had Price, http://www.nytimes.com/2008/01/22/us/politics/22giuliani.html

make it through the disaster together. He did not change in that moment and become great; rather he had developed habits along the way that naturally magnified during a difficult time.

Like Mayor Giuliani, early in life, we formed habits that we continued to apply as we matured. Once we continued to exhibit the same habits over and over again, they became patterns of behavior that we took with us into our careers.

What are the habits that differentiate a manager and a leader?

Many of the things that cross your mind when you compare the two are probably similar to what we hear in sessions.

- One tells you what to do, the other listens.
- One requires obedience, the other encourages independent thinking.
- One gives orders, the other provides an example to follow.
- One de-motivates, the other inspires.
- One controls, the other delegates responsibility.

Which one would you rather follow?

CHAPTER 4

The Angel of Darkness or the Angel of Mercy?

Jack Welch, Business Consultant, former CEO of General Electric and Best-Selling Author, overcame a childhood speech impediment to become one of the most influential executives in American business.

"One would never know Jack Welch's childhood was plagued with a stutter. Such an affliction often has an adverse impact on one's future and the person they will become. Though he was unable to rid himself of the stutter until later in his life, he refused to allow his speech impairment to negatively impact his confidence. Welch's mother imbued Jack with the strength and confidence required to perceive his disadvantages in life as largely superficial and to understand that one's limitations are only dictated by their ambition or fear of failure. Although he only stood 5'7", Jack's confidence and self-awareness propelled him to become a determined athlete in his later youth, competing in a variety of sports including hockey and basketball. He was always challenging his personal limits.

"Investing a large amount of time and energy in each sport, Jack did not take defeat easily. After losing one particular hockey game in overtime, Jack became so enraged that he threw his hockey stick across the rink and stormed off. Back in the locker room, Jack and his team were horrified to see his mother burst in intent on teaching her son a much-needed lesson.

Grabbing the collar of Jack's uniform before his team, his mother chastised him, roaring, '*You punk! If you don't know how to lose, you'll never know how to win!*'

"It is this quality which may be most valued in a manager— to never falter in the face of failure but to learn from one's deficiencies in order to improve and to become more resilient. Jack Welch took much of his 'tough guy' demeanor into his career, making him a strong task-focused manager, which contributed to much of the success of GE in the '80s and '90s. Jack's attitude was that he would be the only *manager* at GE. However, he understood that he needed to surround himself with strong *leaders*, and together, this combination would lead to extraordinary results and great success at GE." [12]

Habits can be obstacles in our path or they can help us achieve greater success. The purpose of our leadership process is to help clients discern between habits or patterns of behavior that can contribute or get in the way of our accomplishments. We were hired by a long-term client in the Southeast to work with a particular department within the company. The division's Director was known in the company as a tough and intimidating manager who challenged us to turn this department around in four months or he would "blow it up." He commented (or was it threatened!) as we were leaving his office, "Do not disappoint me." Jokingly, we looked at each other and said, "Leadership is not for the timid."

Our short-term plan included a diagnostic study of the department's issues, a four-segment leader development process and coaching for the management team...we united, we hit our targets, we celebrated, and we lived to fight another day! And isn't that really what this game we are playing is all about?

---

[12] McKay R., 2013. How a boy with a stutter became the titan who transformed General Electric and defined American ingenuity – Jack Welch in Perspective, http://blog.ceo.ca/2013/05/03/jack-welch/

Our path to success with this department was changing the habits of the management team as a whole. One of the managers we coached during this process was a guy from a small town in New Jersey. His view of the world was limited to the several blocks he grew up in and his experiences from this specific blue-collar neighborhood. As a result, he developed certain communication, social, and even survival habits that he took with him for years to come. He further solidified his narrow view and learned behaviors by joining the Navy. He developed bonds with a group of sailors who all shared the same rough, tough, rugged view of the world. His skills served him well in his youth and in the Navy.

However, when he took those views into a more diverse professional career, his limited view did not serve him so well. In fact, it exposed a number of deficiencies. He worked with a team who perceived him as lacking diplomacy, unable to listen to others, barking orders with an expectation of compliance, avoiding eye contact, and speaking at a rapid pace. This resulted in a lack of trust and respect for him, causing discord among the team.

After an awareness of his behavior and the impact on those around him, we subsequently encouraged him to focus on habits that helped the team versus those that hindered or would get in the way of success. After identifying the habits that were obstacles, we discussed ways to move out of his natural comfort zone to establish new habits, because what comes naturally can sometimes be self-defeating.

For others to believe we have changed, they must see consistency in our behavior. It does not happen overnight or from changing our reaction to one incident but must continue to be observed over time.

We must keep building and focusing on sustaining the behavior change, one step at a time, each and every day. It's like losing weight. If we focus on losing 10 pounds at once it becomes overwhelming, so we focus instead on losing one rogue pound at a time. Then we focus on losing the next pound, and the next, until we have achieved our target. Like waves on a beach, old habits have a way of sneaking back into our daily routine. We want to stick with it until the unnatural behavior becomes natural.

Managers often neglect to recognize a need to change and will continue to exhibit what is easy or what comes naturally. In contrast, *leaders* are aware of the changing internal and external environment, which reminds them to revisit habits to determine if they are still relevant or need to be adjusted.

For example, Tom Skains, former President and CEO of Piedmont Natural Gas, said that once he reached the executive level in the organization, he became more aware of his responses and behavioral habits. He realized that he did not have the luxury of having a bad day at the office. He understood that employees are always observing his leadership, and his tone and behavior could affect everyone in the organization.

The type of leader, one that is able to adapt and adopt new habits to strengthen their leadership behavior, is the difference in a team that is able to move forward as a unified force. Leadership is not necessarily a tangible thing, but it leads to tangible results. Therefore, the value of leadership development to companies is priceless.

Management and leadership…both are essential dynamics in the workplace in order to be successful, but we need to know when and how to use each dynamic effectively.

✤

Management is not leadership, but leadership includes management.

✤

Let's take a closer look at both management and leadership. We believe there are only six viable patterns of management and leadership behaviors that exist. We all tend to gravitate toward one of them.

- Three pivot toward tasks - mostly management characteristics: the **Apollyon, Sentinel,** and **Criterion.**
- Two pivot mostly toward people - more leadership qualities: the **Strategist** and **Synergist.**
- The balance of both management and leadership is **The Actualizer.**

There is one additional pattern, **Aberrant**, that is not a viable option for management or leadership because it is divisive, destructive, and debilitating. We will address all of these patterns throughout the book. Let's begin by looking at the two opposite extremes of pure task-focused management and purely people-focused leadership behavior patterns. Realize, though, that too much of either one can be counterproductive.

≈

**We like to use the analogy of balancing a scale.
The complete opposite behavior patterns - task-focused versus people-oriented - are noted on the next page, and the goal is to find the appropriate balance without being weighted too far toward either side.**

≈

Apollyon
Power &
Control
Solo
Player
Dismissive
Everything
is Black &
White -
no gray areas
Bottom line!
Intimidating
& Threatening
Reactive
Crisis Manager

Synergist
Facilitates
vs. Leads
Consensus vs.
Decisive
Goes-Along-
to-Get-Along
Avoids Conflict
Easygoing
Likable
Social
Harmonious
Generous to a
Fault

The Angel of Darkness

The Apollyon, literally defined as the Prince of Darkness, is a pure manager, with very little, if any, leadership skills. The Synergist is affectionately referred to as the Angel of Mercy and is a pure people-pleaser with very little, if any, management skills.

Synergist stands for a person that cooperates with others to enhance an effect on an outcome, whereas the Apollyon is an independent player, making solo decisions based on one's own knowledge and experience. The goal is to find a balance between the two.

For those who have difficulty believing that pure Apollyon behavior exists in the workplace, study Jack Welch. He referred to one division that he ran prior to becoming the CEO, as "mummies" in an article in Fortune Magazine in August of 1984, and the month prior had been named the toughest boss in America on *Fortune's* Top 10 Toughest Bosses list in which *"being autocratic, ruthless, grueling and intimidating were qualifications for the title."*

Apollyons' interactions with others are often demeaning, humiliating, and border on cruelty. They display an abrupt and cutting sense of humor that is sarcastic and usually offensive. The constant loud, profane, and negative verbal warfare is often used as a form of control and intimidation.

We were talking about this pattern in one of our sessions and we mentioned the name of an Apollyon we believe to be one of the toughest Apollyons we had ever met - and we have met our fair share. One person in the room quickly ran out of the room in tears. When we spoke to her later, she said she had worked for the person we mentioned. Ten years later just hearing his name reminded her of the *"footprints he left on her back."*

There are two primary reasons Apollyons are promoted to higher-level positions. First and foremost, they are relentlessly driven to achieve bottom-line results whatever the cost. As long as they achieve those results, companies are tolerant of their aggressive behavior and will look the other way. However, Apollyons know if they stumble or fail to meet the numbers, the organization will quickly lose its tolerance and will remove them from their position.

Apollyons will work around the clock if they have to in order to achieve their goal and expect others to do the same.

Yahoo CEO Marissa Mayer would *"literally work 24 hours a day, 7 days a week."* According to Business Insider's July 2012 issue. *New York Magazine*, described Mayer as dismissive of people who *"want eight hours of sleep a night, three meals a day."*[13] *Entrepreneur* Magazine commented, she *"thinks sleep is for the weak."*[14]

---

[13] L. Miller, Love and War, 2012. Can Marissa Mayer Really Have It All? https://www.thecut.com/2012/10/marissa-mayer-yahoo-ceo.html

[14] Entis, L., 2015. Mysterious Marissa Mayer: 5 Things You Might Not Know About the Yahoo CEO, https://www.entrepreneur.com/article/2

The second reason Apollyons are often successful is they are effective crisis managers because they are warriors and a crisis is their war. Apollyons have detached themselves emotionally from people. People become objects or things. This detachment makes it easy for them to make the tough calls quickly during a crisis. Most of us agonize over making difficult decisions, such as firing or laying off employees, demanding a punishing work schedule or closing facilities, which leads to sleepless nights. However, the Apollyon will push people to the limit with grueling work schedules and make snap decisions without forethought. They will fire five, fifty or 500 people and still sleep comfortably that night.

Early in Rick's career, he worked for a large North Carolina based bank. There was a guy named Harry who was brought in by the president as a last resort after trying everything reasonable to turn a bad situation around. The employees referred to him as "Dirty Harry." Sometimes, the mere mention of his name and the possibility that he was coming in, would cause a department to turn itself around. Harry was a crisis manager and if there was a way to salvage a department, he was the one who could do it. But Harry would remind the president, if he could not turn it around in a certain amount of time, he was going to *"blow up every damn one of them and leave God to sort it out."*

Apollyons are very effective at resolving a crisis. They can make the tough decisions quickly and without remorse.

However, the caution with the Apollyon is that they create a crisis-driven environment. They are extremely impatient.

Everything is urgent, and the Apollyon is continually reacting. This constant crisis-mode is exhausting and unproductive. The operating environment moves from one pressing dilemma to another, project-to-project, idea to idea, and is constantly changing direction. Everything is a priority to the Apollyon, which leads to confusion, lack of focus, uncertainty, bordering on chaos. In other words, you are in a perpetual world of clutter. If you work for an Apollyon, you work hard, feel under constant siege and stress all day long, yet feel like you've accomplished nothing. When a real crisis arises, everything is intensified, and they become even more demanding and controlling.

Once the crisis has ended, Apollyons begin to push blame. Even though they may have been the one who created the crisis, they will still find a way to transfer the fault to others. Apollyons go on the hunt to find someone to be the "fall guy." Everyone is in the crosshairs until they find the target. Over time, this behavior can create turnover, damage morale, and ultimately hinder performance.

The reality is Apollyons are part of every work environment and we have to find a way to co-exist with them. There are a range of issues and methods for working with an Apollyon that we review in our leadership sessions. However, we want to provide a glimpse of how you can better interact with them.

Apollyons have a black or white view of the world. If we start rationalizing, explaining or giving "I think" answers, it can become ugly very quickly because they have no tolerance for gray areas. When meeting with an Apollyon, have a get-in and get-out mentality, be time aware, no casual conversation about the weather, football game or weekend. Be concise, to the point, and tie everything to the bottom-line. They will challenge your idea and position and take the opposite view, even if they agree with your viewpoint, to draw you into a verbal debate and test your resolve. Do not engage. Stay on point and don't take the bait.

Show no fear or doubt, do not waiver or they will consider it a weakness and attack with verbal combat. They are better at that game than the rest of us.

Match strength on strength.
Their strength is intimidation and threat.
Our strength is our conviction and belief in our message.

ى

The Other Extreme: The Angel of Mercy

The previous pattern was virtually all task and little, if any, people consideration. However, The Angel of Mercy - the Synergist - is all about people and less about task. A Synergist is a person who cooperates to achieve a harmonious outcome, a synergy or teamwork over the individual.

Synergists, in essence, are a safe sanctuary for others. They will take on the weight of others' problems. They will take an inordinate amount of time to listen and genuinely show concern. They are so caught up in care and consideration for others that the emphasis becomes the people, not the task itself. Often, the focus on people and their feelings expose them as a weak manager. Their significant attention to people overshadows their interest in accomplishing a task.

Outside of a business setting, however, Synergists are humanitarians who put people above all else. There is great strength in this. Do not confuse weakness with kindness.

Synergists have an inner strength where they will take a stand for a cause they believe in, even to the point of sacrificing themselves. Synergists believe you can kill the messenger, but never the message.

Nelson Mandela was a South African anti-apartheid revolutionary, politician, and philanthropist, who served as President of South Africa from 1994 to 1999. He was sentenced to life imprisonment in 1964 as an activist for the African National Congress (ANC). Released in 1990, he was awarded the Nobel Peace Prize (1993).

He was willing to sacrifice his own freedom to take the peoples' side.

> *"For to be free is not merely to cast off one's chains,*
> *but to live in a way that respects and enhances the*
> *freedom of others.* - **Nelson Mandela**

Mother Teresa founded the Order of Missionaries of Charity, noted for its work among the poor in Kolkata (Calcutta). She was also awarded the Nobel Peace Prize (1979). Tom Hafer shared a well-known story in Faith and Fitness,

> *"As she was working with severely needy children,*
> *a reporter told Mother Teresa, 'I wouldn't do what*
> *you're doing for a million dollars.' She simply but*
> *profoundly replied, 'neither would I.'"[15]*

In a philanthropic sense, this is admirable and self-sacrificing, however, in a business sense, Synergists often over-extend themselves for the benefit of others and become personally involved with the concerns of co-workers. They place a high priority on people and their well-being, avoiding confrontation and conflict. They will continue to "go-along-to-get-along" rather than make waves in the office. Realize that too much agreement is just as deadly to an organization as too much conflict.

ᘒ

Synergists with their need to please can lead to mediocrity.

ᘒ

Without complete consensus, Synergists can't easily make decisions. They begin to overanalyze those decisions and delay until the opportunity vanishes or until they defer to the team.

---

[15] Klein, T, 2017, What Mother Teresa Wouldn't Do for a Million Dollars (commonly used quote), https://www.americamagazine.org/faith/2017/02/02/what-mother-teresa-wouldnt-do-million-dollars

This can hurt the ability to consider other opinions, options, and alternatives. They also lose the healthy debate that can help a team reach a better outcome or find a better solution to a problem.

On the other hand, Synergists are also the conscience of the organization and are mindful of the implications and the impact decisions may have on the employees' well-being.

Synergists will diligently remind management of the consequences decisions and actions can have on employees. However, the reality is that the tougher decisions almost always involve people and may likely have negative consequences for them. Synergists will procrastinate and prolong these types of decisions as long as possible, which is often counter-productive to the organization or team.

We were thinking about examples of Synergists who were great leaders. All of our examples were humanitarians who changed the world, some of whom we mentioned above with Mother Teresa and Nelson Mandela. However, none were business leaders. After perusing the Internet to find a business Synergist leader to offer to you, we came to the conclusion that it is rare, or perhaps non-existent, to find a Synergist who is a great business leader. We did finally stumble on a blog by Ron Edmondson, Pastor and Church Consultant on leadership issues, who captured the essence of the Synergist operating style:

> *"[Sarah] is an incredibly kind and gentle person. She's smart, hard-working, and loyal…In talking through the specific situation, it quickly became obvious she had one weakness and it was affecting her entire team. It's a common weakness among leaders. At times, most of us will struggle in this area. Her weakness?* **She was being too nice!**
>
> *I realize this doesn't sound like it could ever be a weakness. It has made her well-liked in the*

organization. She's incredibly popular and, she likes that. But, it also made her team less successful than it could have been. Thankfully, she recognized it but wasn't sure how to fix it. A few team members were taking advantage of her agreeable nature by under-performing in their role. She hadn't challenged the problems even though she knew she should. She was losing sleep over it but didn't know what to do. The relational leadership in her, which is a positive aspect in her leadership style, was not working for these team members."

Pastor Ron continued, "Perhaps you've seen this before in an organization. Maybe you've been on either side of this issue. I am not suggesting one become a mean leader; it would be wrong. I am suggesting one become a wise leader. Wisdom guides people in the direction that is best for them, the leader, and the entire team or organization ... Are you allowing problems to continue out of a fear of not being liked? There is nothing wrong with being a relational (Synergist) leader. That can be a great style of leadership, but part of developing any healthy relationship involves conflict, tough conversations and difficult decisions."

ے

If you are not careful, you can become everyone's friend, but nobody's leader.

ے

"Leading is hard – some days harder than others. The sooner you handle the problem (and the problem people), the sooner things will begin to improve on your team for everyone – and the sooner you can get a good night's rest."

Synergists procrastinate and refrain from confronting problems in timely, truthful and decisive ways. They fear losing the approval of those around them if they are confrontational. The irony is, the opposite is true. Issues must be addressed with honesty and conviction to gain the respect of others.

Trying to create a safe harbor, Synergists may find themselves docked at the Port of Indecision, where few, if any, ships ever sail. Organizations typically overlook or only give minor attention to, the lack of timeliness and accomplishment of the Synergist since they tend to fly under the radar in a quiet, polite, encouraging fashion rather than making waves and creating a visible problem. It is a peaceful disruption but can be frustrating to those who work with them.

In other words, even though the relational side of the equation is positive, it must be combined with the management-task side as well. The key to success is to combine the two dynamics appropriately, and bring management or a task focus to the table without the meanness of the Apollyon, along with consideration for others without overcompensating the people side at the expense of results like the Synergist.

Think About...

The Synergist idealistic view of the world, that of goodness, becomes blurred when translated into the reality of the world of business.

"The only way three people can keep a secret is if two of them are dead." - **Al Capone**

CHAPTER 5

The Godfather, The Consigliere, and The Rogue Player

The three patterns in this chapter are the patterns between the purely task-focused and purely people-focused patterns discussed in the last chapter. There is a bit more blending of tasks and people in these patterns but with a clear pivot one way or the other. These patterns include:

- The Godfather **(Sentinel)** who requires respect and loyalty.

- The meticulous analytical bookkeeper, the Consigliere **(Criterion)**, who is loyal, follows orders, lives by the rules, and has knowledge of every detail of the business.

- The flamboyant Rogue Player **(Strategist)** who draws attention to their grandiose ideas and talkative nature.

The Godfather or **Boss** is also known as the **Sentinel**, meaning one who stands as if watching (e.g. watching over the family). The Godfather is ego-driven toward a position of influence and seeks attention and recognition for achievements. The Sentinel/ Godfather seeks prestige over money and greater influence over power. However, they often have money and power by virtue of their position of influence.

The Sentinel views those who report to them as their family team. Respect, trust, and loyalty are the cornerstones of those relationships. Honoring those codes is not an option; it is a requirement for membership in the family. In other words, the team is valued above all else and if you break any of the family/ team codes, you are no longer worthy and will suffer the consequences. Once you have lost your "membership," it is tough, if not virtually impossible, to regain access.

The consequence for real or perceived disloyalty can be a "hand slap" in the form of removing benefits you have previously enjoyed, such as attending association meetings in exotic locations or being assigned the best clients. However, it can also be as extreme as being removed from your position. When working with this pattern, these codes need to be clearly understood.

However, the Sentinel does offer a quid-pro-quo when you are loyal in the form of rewards to those who demonstrate allegiance. Perhaps this comes in the form of a promotion and entrusting you with increased responsibility or as gifts for your family (e.g. tickets to the ball game or a nice dinner for you and your spouse, etc.).

✌

**Any indication of disloyalty can
be detrimental to your career.**

✌

Sentinels use an implied power, whereas, Apollyons use an overt, loud, and noisy in-your-face power. This implied power is used to enforce discipline and order on the team. They understand that implied power is more influential than applying power.

> *"Real power is having it but not having to use it."*
> **- Schindler's List**

The Sentinel would address the team, "*It is imperative we achieve our targets this quarter, and for those who produce the results, the sky is the limit.*" In other words, the team knows what the Sentinel wants, how they want it, when they want it, and what is implied if they do not get it.

In the book "*On Wings of Eagles*" by Ken Follett, Billionaire Ross Perot was quoted as saying he created "*the biggest jailbreak*" in history. Two of his employees in Iran were taken hostage. Perot put together his own Commando team to fly over and get them out. He felt he owed it to the two men and their families since they had been with him in the beginning when he borrowed $1,000 from his wife to start Electronic Data Systems (EDS). This is an example of the quid-pro-quo of the Sentinel.

However, the opposite was true as well. It was said that if your picture was on the wall for making Employee of the Year and you resigned, Ross Perot would have your picture removed from the wall for essentially committing the ultimate act of betrayal.

Sentinels value traditional business strategies and take pride in teaching and preserving those methods. Decisions are influenced by custom and cultural time-honored values. The Sentinel will look for someone who has a level-headed tone, appropriate restraint, and a seasoned approach. They want to know that the ideas, strategy or plans have been completely thought through along with the consequences of the actions. Sentinels do not like surprises nor do they want to draw negative attention to themselves or the team.

They will go through the motions of getting input, but typically only as a formality, because they have likely already made the decision. They also seek input as a loyalty check to make sure others agree with their viewpoint. Independent thinking can be interpreted as not fully buying into their position, which can have a detrimental cost.

If a team member believes the Sentinel is going down an incorrect path, options and alternatives must be provided, which also should include the Sentinel's idea as one of the recommendations. The presentation should package the preferred path as having the greater rewards or benefits and should help guide or persuade the Sentinel to the team member's option.

However, the Godfather must make the final choice and support must be exhibited for whichever idea is chosen. Their trusted team members or "lieutenants," carry out their plans without questioning authority. As loyalty is demonstrated, a positive relationship ensues. Using language such as, "I will take care of it," and "Done," are necessary.

≈

**Always keep the Sentinel informed of progress
to foster the relationship. No surprises.**

≈

Sentinels can even be identified by their appearance. They dress traditionally and immaculately in a designer suit. They carry an air of sophistication, formality, and protocol that causes you to sit up a little straighter in their presence. Think of a lawyer in the courtroom, always dressed immaculately to impress.

A Midwest company hired me to coach an Executive VP in the company. This particular person was Apollyon, the toughest of the tough. This is the most unlikely pattern to make any sustainable change in behavior, especially in this case where I was asked to come in as a last resort. I felt like the priest being called in to give last rights. However, the President of the company and this Executive were friends outside of work and their families would get together on various occasions. They had worked together for many years.

Be that as it may, the complaints were becoming too frequent to ignore. Therefore, I was brought in to "change him." Once I met with the Executive VP, I was ushered into the President's massive, plush office and shown a seat. The President was sitting behind his completely organized, neat, and tidy mahogany desk that had only one file folder open and in front of him. The office created an aura of formality with wall-to-wall carpet and large windows. It was an exquisitely decorated office with the furniture arranged to perfection, and there was a picture on the desk of him shaking hands with the mayor. I was seated in a chair in front of this enormous desk.

Once he finished reviewing his notes, he stood up, put on his coat complete with red, silk handkerchief in the pocket, and came around to my side of the desk. I knew I was in the presence of the Godfather. I remember his hair was immaculately combed back and his dark pinstriped expensive suit fit as if tailor-made. I stood up and he shook my hand, gesturing for me to sit back down. Fully expecting him to sit in the chair next to me, I was surprised to see him sit on the edge of his desk, essentially hovering over me. I immediately sat up straighter and made sure I addressed him as "sir." I listened intently when he spoke.

In his imposing position of authority, he began to ask me questions about my conversation with his Executive. He was engaging with a formality that spoke of his expectations. Of course, I only spoke when asked a question and I answered honestly and respectfully. When he was ready to end the conversation, he said, *"Make sure you keep me fully informed and tell me everything about your conversations with [Ben]moving forward."* Of course, I did.

Our conversations with clients are always confidential unless given permission to share. I made sure the Executive understood anything he said could be used against him, and as a stereotypical Apollyon, he didn't care. Initially, the Executive took measures to follow the advice of his Sentinel boss, but ultimately fell back into his old Apollyon disruptive habits and was asked to "retire."

An important side note to mention is that, around the same time, the company decided to start a creative "think tank" in the business to help them stay viable and competitive. They had the new team report directly to this same Sentinel President of the company. The creative department was doomed before it started. The Godfather would not allow them to implement any of their ideas because they were contrary to his more traditional viewpoints and conventional wisdom regarding how the family should operate and "do business."

Always remember, within the family, the Godfather-Sentinel *is* the "final solution" to the problem. In contrast, when the Sentinel is dealing outside the family/team with others of similar authority, they will work with the other heads of the family, or departments, to find a peaceful solution to the problem and unify together. However, if someone breaks that bond or contract, the Sentinel has other means of covertly undermining, or even removing, the person from the inner circle.

**The Sentinel's method of operation
is always covert, never overt.**

The Consigliere and The Rogue Player

These two patterns are so prevalent in the workplace that a full understanding of how they think could make all the difference in success. One thinks at ground level and the other thinks 20,000 feet above the boundaries. These two patterns drive each other crazy but desperately need one another. One comes up with the big ideas and the other carries them out. Strategists/Rogue Players are elegant thinkers and speakers, able to communicate their grandiose ideas in a mesmerizing manner. Whereas, Criterions/ Consigliere are factual, precise, and deliver in a monotone, methodical fashion, without eliciting the enthusiasm of the Strategist.

However, the Criterion's information is usually correct and without embellishment or exaggeration, while the Strategist tends toward the opposite. It is not because Strategists are deliberately being untruthful, but rather, they simply get caught up in their own dreams and ideas. The minnow sometimes grows larger until it's portrayed as a fifteen-pound bass!

In other words, with a Criterion, we can typically rely on the accuracy of their information. With a Strategist the information should not be taken fully at face value, but rather the suggestion would be to fact-check their sources. One has more substance while the other has more sizzle.

SIZZLE:

Sir Richard Charles Nicholas Branson is an English business magnate, investor, and philanthropist who founded the Virgin Group, which controls more than 400 companies. Branson expressed his desire to become an entrepreneur at the young age of sixteen, with his first business venture, a magazine called *Student*. In 1970, he set up a mail-order record business, and in 1972, he opened a chain of record stores called Virgin Records, later known as Virgin Megastores.

Branson's Virgin brand grew rapidly during the 1980s as he set up Virgin Atlantic airline and expanded the Virgin Records music label. In March 2000, Branson was knighted at Buckingham Palace for "services to entrepreneurship" for his work in retail, music, and transport interests spanning land, air, sea, and space travel. With his taste for adventure and his humanitarian work, he became one of the most prominent figures in British culture. In 2002, he was named in the BBC's poll of the 100 Greatest Britons. In January 2016, Forbes listed Branson's estimated net worth at $5.2 billion.[16]

The following are excerpts from the Forbes Magazine, September 23, 2014, interview with Dan Schawbel, that clearly shows Branson with classic characteristics of the Strategist.

> **Dan Schawbel:** *How would you describe your leadership style? How do you believe this style makes your company culture unique?*

[16] Wikipedia

Richard Branson: *Rule-breaker, because I never learned the rules in the first place. To change the game is at the heart of what Virgin stands for, so the company culture has always been: Don't sweat it: rules were meant to be broken. The commitment is about doing things differently.*

Schawbel: *How did you originally come up with Virgin's values, vision, and mission, then find the right people who believed in you and the company?*

Branson: *The Virgin values have and will always be the same: to change the game and challenge the status quo by providing a product or service of great use...Along the way, we saw gaps in the market where Virgin could play a role and be an incredible force for good, and that's become our motto. Our strategy has been to screw business as usual.* [17]

SUBSTANCE:

Roger Boisjoly was a booster rocket engineer at NASA in January 1986, when he and four colleagues became embroiled in the fatal decision to launch the Space Shuttle Challenger. Boisjoly was one of two confidential sources quoted by NPR three weeks later in the first detailed report about the Challenger launch decision and the stiff resistance by Boisjoly and other Thiokol engineers. The experience both haunted and inspired Boisjoly in the decades that followed.

Bulky, bald, and tall, Boisjoly was an imposing figure, especially when armed with data. He found disturbing data about the booster rockets that would lift Challenger into space. Six months

---

[17] Schawbel, D., 2014. Richard Branson's Three Most Important Leadership Principles, https://www.forbes.com/sites/danschawbel/2014/09/23/richard-branson-his-3-most-important-leadership-principles/#701fb5933d50

before the Challenger explosion, he predicted: *"a catastrophe of the highest order"* involving *"loss of human life"* in a memo to managers at Thiokol. The problem, Boisjoly wrote, was the elastic seals at the joints of the multi-stage booster rockets.

They tended to stiffen and unseal in cold weather and NASA's ambitious shuttle launch schedule included winter lift-offs with risky temperatures.[18]

On January 27, 1986, the forecast for the next morning at the Kennedy Space Center in Florida, included a launch-time temperature as low as 30 degrees Fahrenheit. NASA had never launched in temperatures that cold and Boisjoly and his four colleagues at Thiokol headquarters in Utah concluded it would be too dangerous to launch. *"We all knew what the implication was without actually coming out and saying it,"* a tearful Boisjoly told NPR's Zwerdling in 1986. *"We all knew if the seals failed the shuttle would blow up."*

Armed with the data that described that possibility, Boisjoly and his colleagues argued persistently and vigorously for hours. At first, Thiokol managers agreed with them and formally recommended a launch delay. But NASA officials challenged that recommendation. One source told us that pressure from NASA caused Thiokol managers to *"put their management hats on."* They overruled Boisjoly and the other engineers and told NASA to go ahead and launch.

So, when Challenger lifted off without incident, he and the others watching the television screens at Thiokol's Utah plant were relieved.

---

[18] NPR, *All Things Considered,* Feb. 6, 2012 broadcast, Roger Boisjoly: He Tried to Stop Shuttle Challenger Launch.

"When we were one minute into the launch, a friend turned to me and said, 'Oh God. We made it. We made it!'" Boisjoly continued. *"Then, a few seconds later, the shuttle blew up and we all knew exactly what happened."*

The explosion of Challenger and the deaths of its crew, including a school teacher, Christa McAuliffe, traumatized the nation and left Boisjoly disabled by severe headaches, steeped in depression, and unable to sleep. Boisjoly testified before the Challenger Commission and filed unsuccessful lawsuits against Thiokol and NASA.

Boisjoly wrestled daily with an issue that all scientists fear, but few have to face: When does one speak out? And at what price to one's career and to one's company? Ultimately, Boisjoly spoke up and became the outcast who caused problems with too many facts and too much knowledge of what happened with the Challenger. He became the fall guy that was symbolically eliminated.

I trust Jesus. Everyone else, bring me the data.

Criterion literally describes a standard of judgment or set of criteria by which they measure everything. They often find themselves in an advisory capacity because of the abundance of information they gather and process, just like Boisjoly took his criteria, or data, to management to advise them to delay the launch. The data is used to rationalize, explain and point out consequences. They find security in detail, analysis, and numbers. They measure success, not necessarily by moving up the ladder, but by perfecting their job, and to Criterions data is irrefutable. Nothing is intuitive without the data and that is the impetus that drives everything they do. Their decisions and actions are the results of a rigid focus on detail and precision. Often, they are promoted due to their attention to detail and accuracy when completing a task.

The dilemma is that they are promoted for their task orientation and expertise, but lack the charisma, flexibility, and diplomacy that would move them into the higher-level positions in an organization. The relationship side is challenging for them and outside their comfort zone. They have the task focus and management needed for bringing discipline and structure to an organization but lack the people-focus and leadership that must be equally present for ultimate success. Some of the Criterion traits include:

- Finding security in the status quo.
- Knowing what they like; liking what they know.
- Preferring things to stay the same and be predictable and comfortable.
- Resisting and challenging change.
- Having the perspective, "if it ain't broke, don't fix it."

Criterions are task-focused and detail-oriented, which often leads to a very efficient and highly disciplined work environment. However, this pattern can be viewed as inflexible due to their propensity for strictly following rules and regulations.

One of our clients revealed that she knew she had similar tendencies when she was going to lunch one day and saw someone from her building jaywalking instead of using the crosswalk. She chased him down and suggested he use the crosswalk moving forward as it is mandated by the company regulations. After lunch, she noticed the same individual jaywalking again back to the office. She confronted him a second time about his blatant disregard for following rules. She then spent the next two weeks trying to find his manager, so she could report him for not following company policy and crossing at the designated crosswalks.

Think of all the time and cost lost to the company while she spent two weeks focused on the wrong thing. Rules are there for a reason, but at what point does it become evident we have crossed the line and let the rules become the master, which can end up defeating the very purpose for which the rule was intended?

To their credit, Criterions provide structure, discipline, and order to the organization. However, their vision does not extend beyond their methodical, systematic, procedural way of doing things, which is a narrow view of the world. If there are any interruptions to that way of doing things, it immobilizes them. They move into paralysis-analysis and can't make decisions or move forward. They become hyper-focused on the "hair on the elephant's butt," and miss the elephant entirely.

Criterions believe in evolution not revolution, letting things evolve over time versus big changes at one time. The best way to get them to buy into a change and minimize resistance, keep them involved in the implementation part of the process. The more involved the Criterions are in the change process, the more they keep their sense of security. Then they will accomplish a task accurately, according to policy and procedures. Inclusion allows them to have influence over the process, which provides comfort with making the change.

Derek Villanueva, Sales Manager of Major and National Accounts for The Oklahoman Media Company in Oklahoma City, OK, attended one of our leadership sessions. He was primarily a Criterion, very analytical, status-quo and conventional-oriented. This combination can often lead to procrastination on decisions due to getting paralyzed by the details and losing the ability to rationalize a situation, impeding progress.

Prior to attending our session, Derek felt he had been working every day within a safety zone, which resulted in a limited view of how to deal with issues. Our session helped him achieve an expanded view and range of alternatives that led to a broader perspective of how to interact with others and increase flexibility that would lead to greater success. Understanding the patterns of behavior provided an increased level of self-awareness and the ability to break through those narrow boundaries.

Four years later, as we were facilitating one of our ongoing programs with The Oklahoman Media Company, Derek surprised us with a visit to announce his second promotion in the company and credited his advancement directly to attending our session.

ॐ

"This was the most impactful development process of my career," said Derek Villanueva. "It provided insights I could immediately apply."

ॐ

The Rogue Player

Sincerity is the key to success. Once you can fake that, everything else is easy.

The opposite view would be Strategists/Rogue Players who are good at selling their concepts, strategies, and plans. Think of them as elegant thinkers, always finding ways to persuade others to join their viewpoint and buy into their ideas. A distinct but subtle difference between a **Strategic Thinker** (see chapter 6) and a **Strategist** is that the strategic thinker encourages creative ideas from others but always brings it back to what makes sense for the team or organization. A Strategist, however, believes it is less fun at lower altitudes, so they are always thinking 20,000 feet above the status quo. Strategists are creative and innovative. They challenge our companies to move to the next level in a savvy and persuasive manner that can sometimes be perceived as manipulation.

It is like a chess game where the pieces are always moving around the chessboard as they try to out-think, out-maneuver, and out-strategize their opponent. They have a way of capturing our imagination as we dream and live their dreams. That is how Strategists draw us into their view and gain our buy-in. They thrive on doing things differently and carry us with them on the journey. Their energy and enthusiasm for taking risks with innovative ideas often leads the Strategist to success but can be overwhelming to the more conservative individuals.

Strategists are visionary and a bit quixotic (idealistic dreamers) as they often lack details to accompany their creative ideas. To compensate for the lack of interest in details, they will leave the specifics and execution of the plan to others. They are not delegating for developmental purposes, but rather dumping the details onto someone else, typically the Criterion pattern. They believe this trivia is far too ground level or mundane.

Strategists love a challenge. They are extroverts with a competitive drive. They are liked by clients and are generally good company representatives. They enjoy brainstorming meetings, but rarely reach a consensus due to their elusive nature. The team often becomes frustrated with their lack of focus. They also believe it is acceptable to push boundaries to reach a goal, and afterward rationalize any compromise as a valid and necessary means to an end.

One Strategist client that comes to mind loved writing lengthy, self-promoting, and elaborate emails, copying everyone he thought would be impressed by his complex and sophisticated wording. He had a lot to say but didn't consider his audience or their need for the information. Every email was an extravagant novel that no one had the time or patience to read. When questioned, his response was he *"liked writing that way."* He enjoyed writing and talking in eloquent terms to get us to believe the latest idea he was selling. However, he often ended up rambling and off-topic, diluting the message, and frustrating the recipients.

With a Strategist, it is all about image. Pinning a Strategist down to a definitive answer or decision is like negotiating with Jello. They are intentionally ambiguous and elusive. We recommend telling them your opinion and asking their input, knowing that you will leave with a vague response. Then you do whatever you believe to be right, and as long as you make them "look good" to others, they will move on to the next big thing.

A Gamble in the Sand
The Transformation of Las Vegas

The 1940s brought big changes for Las Vegas, especially after federal and local authorities in Los Angeles began cracking down on illegal gambling circuits running booze, broads, and betting. Many of these shaken gamblers and gangsters sought refuge in Nevada. Two of those displaced gangsters, Meyer Lansky and Benjamin "Bugsy" Siegel, endured the hot, slow trip to Las Vegas in a Cadillac, where Lansky envisioned Las Vegas as a future gambling magnet.[19]

> *"The winners are those who control the game,"*
> *Lansky said. "All the rest are suckers."*

Then on December 26, 1946, the Flamingo Hotel, conceived by Hollywood reporter and gambler, Billy Wilkerson, built with mob money, opened to underwhelming reviews.

The place was designed as the haute destination for high rollers, unlike the Old West theme pervading other Las Vegas casinos at the time. Heavy losses at its opening caused the Flamingo to close, reopening in March of 1947. This time, like so many Las Vegas success stories to come, the joint turned a profit by the end of the month. But when Siegel was murdered at his girlfriend's Beverly Hills mansion, a tsunami of publicity washed over Las Vegas. Americans began to see what Lansky and Siegel had out in the desert and that Las Vegas was an edgy, glamorous place to be.

---

19 Manning, M. and Samuelson, A., 2008. *How Las Vegas transformed itself from a railroad watering hole to the 'Entertainment Capital of the World.'*

The oasis in the desert that was developed called Las Vegas came largely from the Strategist vision of two notorious mobsters.

Due to the Strategists enterprising character, they will bring the future to our organizations.

The reality is that people are different, and we will be working alongside each of these patterns of behavior.

The Strategist talks above the crowd and the room noise, in a boastful manner, draws a lot of attention and is difficult to trust. They are a little too independent and act on their own, all of which are potentially detrimental to their career, especially if they work for the Sentinel.

The Criterion is loyal, follows orders, and lives by the rules. But when things get "hot," will the bookkeeper be the whistleblower?

- Does the Strategist talk too much?
- Does the Criterion know too much?
- Do you ever really know where you stand with the Sentinel?

> All we know is Al Capone said, *"The only way three people can keep a secret is if two of them are dead."*

❧

It doesn't mean these relationships can't work, it just means that each of them has to *work* at the relationship!

❧

The Case of the Two GMs

In a 1994 article, *Leading Your Positively Outrageous Service Team*, service consultant, T. Scott Gross, shares an ad that impressed him:

> *"We blew a deadline, ticked everyone off, cost the company a bundle, and we did the right thing," said Jim Perkins. "What if you ran a division of General Motors and were due to debut an important flagship model and it wasn't quite ready? Nothing drastic you understand, just a few glitches that meant not every car coming off the line was just right. What if you'd sworn to your bosses you'd be ready? What if you had a lot of potential customers waiting to get a first look? What would you do?*

Here is what Jim Perkins and his team did: they pulled the plug on the introduction and said, *"When we know we've got it right, we'll bring out the car." That night, Jim Perkins did what people who do the right thing always do. He got a good night's sleep."*

In contrast, a Lieff, Cabraser, Heimann & Bernstein Attorneys at Law newsletter titled, *GM Faulty Ignition Recall*, July 18, 2014, states:

> *"A defect in nearly 6 million GM cars could cause the car's engine and electrical system to shut off and disable the airbags. For a decade, GM and government safety regulators reportedly failed to address this defect, which had been implicated in the deaths of over 300 people in crashes where the front airbags did not deploy. It has been reported*

that GM could have fixed the defective switch for
as little as .57 cents per vehicle."

In the first case, Perkins would not even compromise over a glitch, whereas, the second case involved not only compromising, but compromising with loss of lives. In the first example, Jim Perkins clearly reflects one of the quality characteristics of an Actualizer to measure success. Our last viable behavior pattern, **Actualizers,** do not interpret the line, they define the line.

CHAPTER 6

The Strength of Management, The Influence of Leadership

Enron was one of the largest corporations in America until it collapsed after accounting and corporate fraud was discovered among the most senior level officials. They hid the financial losses of the trading business and other operations of the company. It was the biggest corporate bankruptcy to ever hit the financial world at that time.

In Gulf of Mexico, British Petroleum tried to cover up their catastrophic oil spill, the worst in our nation's history. BP's response was so slow that when the clean-up effort finally began, the oil slick was no longer containable causing great damage to the ecosystem. Then in 2008, there was the financial crisis that led to the worst economy since the great depression. Sadly, the list goes on.

The point is, in every one of the above cases, "leadership" all denied responsibility. They all crossed a line at the expense of people, ecosystems, finances, reputations, and careers. Money trumped all else. When does the violation of trust take precedence over corporate profits? There is often a struggle between our methods and choices of achieving bottom-line results and our own personal set of values. The line blurs and the end can seem to justify the means. Tough decisions almost always involve either people or money…or both. In other words, a brick and mortar decision may be easy, but when people or money are added to the equation, decisions become increasingly complicated. Powerful influences and self-preservation instincts make us all susceptible to compromising our values for the more tangible rewards of money and profits.

*"To some, a lie is nothing more than the truth not
yet revealed."*- **Unknown**

**The Actualizer uses the strength of management and
the influence of leadership in a balanced mix.
They measure success differently.**

Actualizers measure success in two ways. They understand
remaining viable and competitive requires achieving the numbers
and doing what we were hired to do – our job. However, what
defines and separates the Actualizer pattern is how they measure
success by an inner code, equally factoring in corporate and
personal values and balancing both with a focus on achieving
profitability. After Coach K had his 1,000th win at Duke
University, a commentator noted about him,

*"Times change, kids change, recruiting changes. But one thing
that hasn't changed is his values."* It is a code of conduct based
on integrity, honesty, values, ethics, and doing the right thing.
They take a stand with management, service providers, and the
team to achieve success the right way.

ॐ

**"We will hit the numbers, but we will not do it at the
expense of compromising core values."**

ॐ

It is all about ethical choices. The Actualizer has the courage and
conviction to take a position and stand up for what they believe
in.

Kevin Poet, Director of Charlotte Plant Operations with Siemens,
was faced with just such an ethical decision earlier in his career.
At the time, Kevin was responsible for coordinating the delivery,
installation, and launch of all manufacturing process equipment
for Ford Motor Company. They were working with a supplier in

Canada who was well connected to a senior executive within the company, which created an attitude claiming, *"We are the only game in town, and you have to use us."* They arrogantly dismissed Kevin when he showed concern over their lack of responsiveness, late deliveries, and inflated budget.

Kevin had a potentially career-changing decision to make; take on the risk of switching to a smaller company without the same level of capacity and a potentially failed program or continue to work with an unprincipled business partner and overlook the issues. He ultimately decided that if he failed, he was going to fail for the right reasons. Knowing his career was potentially on the line, Kevin chose the new company and stated that they would all succeed, or all fail together. It turned out to be the right decision and the right company.

An ethical issue, or one that disregards a core value of the Actualizer, is a trigger point that will move an Actualizer leader to their more aggressive backup behavior pattern very quickly.

Situational Awareness & Backup Patterns

What we are referring to is that we all have a primary pattern and a backup pattern that we move into when the primary is not working as expected. In our backup pattern, we typically move in a more aggressive direction and exhibit stronger behavior. Each primary behavior pattern has a typical direction they naturally move in for backup.

The Apollyon backup behavior characteristics are intensified to the degree you can feel physically violated. They become more aggressive, intimidating, threatening, and overtly cruel. It can ramp up and eventually lead to a physical attack. It is out-of-control anger and extremely aggressive behavior designed to dominate and obtain absolute control.

The complete opposite is the Synergist who moves into the Criterion's analytical behavior as a delay tactic. This mechanism allows them to procrastinate and delay making a difficult decision, hoping the problem resolves itself. This deliberate move provides an excuse to avoid confronting the tough decisions.

The Boss, or Sentinel, moves to the more dominant behavior of an Apollyon. Sentinels are quite often referred to as dressed-up Apollyons. They have polished the rough edges because they understand that the tough, hard edges of the Apollyon could be harmful to their career. So, when Apollyon action is required, meaning someone must be fired or reprimanded, Sentinels will send in someone else, a lieutenant if you will, to take care of the problem. This allows the Sentinel to maintain their facade of being above reproach.

The Criterion we discussed earlier defaults to an unpredictable pattern, the Aberrant, which is the only non-viable behavior pattern for management and leadership. When Criterions move to Aberrant behavior, they exhibit extreme aggressive conduct or extreme withdrawal resulting in a complete shutdown. Most often when Criterions exhibit this behavior, they are stuck in the analysis mode referred to by psychologists as ruminating or over-thinking. They dis-engage and totally stop communicating or abruptly lash out in anger as a maladaptive coping mechanism to deal with uncomfortable situations or avoid certain people. The Aberrant behavior is not a viable pattern for management or leadership because their erratic behavior is unpredictable and allows them to escape or circumvent the problem rather than deal with it. Leading and managing skills are completely non-existent when avoiding people, tasks, and responsibility.

Before we get too judgmental regarding Aberrant behavior, realize that we have all been guilty of exhibiting this conduct. We have all over-reacted to a situation or individual and we have had moments of simply mentally checking out or retreating to avoid an uncomfortable circumstance. This Aberrant behavior is a natural backup move for the Criterion while for most other patterns it is an anomaly due to severe extenuating circumstances such as loss of a loved one, divorce or being overwhelmed by a particular situation.

Regardless of the reason, we either need to re-align our behavior quickly if this happens or help others on the team who are exhibiting this behavior before it pulls the entire team down... and it will. With limited tolerance, leaders will attempt to coach someone out of the Aberrant behavior. However, they will take action to remove the person from the team before they allow this destructive behavior to spread like a virus and contaminate whole team.

Strategists will move into Sentinel behavior in backup mode. Strategists do not like handling the details, so when pressure increases to provide this level of information, they move to Sentinel and transfer those details to a lieutenant (typically the detailed pattern of the Criterion). This allows the Strategist to stay in their comfort zone and "selling" mode, focusing on the big picture while someone else manages the mundane but necessary substantive information.

The Actualizer has the most situational awareness to provide the greatest range of flexibility, adapt more easily and draw on different behavior patterns to achieve the appropriate results. This pattern knows when to "rent" the other patterns as backup to accomplish a better outcome. Actualizers know when to play the diplomacy card of the Strategist or encourage innovation to think beyond the boundaries and come up with a more creative solution to problems. They know when to focus on details like the Criterion or create a family atmosphere like the Sentinel.

However, when Actualizers need to address more controversial issues or crisis, they have a natural tendency to move to Apollyon behavior without the need for meanness. Rather they increase the sense of urgency, make quicker decisions and hold themselves and others accountable to achieve expedited results.

We feel the heat and intensity of the Apollyon without the intense negativity.

Primary Pattern	Back Up Pattern
Apollyon	Apollyon - extreme/intensified
Synergist	Criterion - paralysis analysis
Sentinel	Apollyon - more dominant
Criterion	Aberrant - lash out or withdraw
Strategist	Sentinel - sends staff to handle issues
Actualizer	Apollyon - increase urgency w/o meanness

The Big Five Triggers

There are five primary trigger points that will cause Actualizers to lose patience and move to backup Apollyon behavior.

The trigger points are:

- compromising a code of honorable behavior
- repeatedly sidestepping ownership of mistakes
- continuing lack of performance
- doing something really, really, really foolish
- being blindsided by a crisis of significant magnitude

The first two are self-explanatory; compromising an ethical code or not taking accountability by blaming someone or something else. The third trigger is important because even though Actualizers will exercise patience with performance-related issues, the patience has limitations since Actualizers are performance-driven high achievers and have an expectation that others are just as conscientious.

Although performance issues frustrate Actualizers, they will partner with us to help strengthen and improve any deficiency so that we, and the team, may be more successful. They will unselfishly give their time and attention to us in a supportive role; whether coaching, directing, training, developing, and/or providing additional resources. However, make no mistake, if after providing this additional support and encouragement the performance bar is still not being met, they will make the tough call and take the necessary steps to remove the under-performer.

The fourth and fifth trigger points necessitate examples to illustrate them more clearly. The fourth, doing something really, really, really foolish is tolerated unless it continues to repeat itself. When this pattern of behavior emerges, the Actualizer begins to question the judgment of the individual, which leads to a confidence issue in the employee's ability to think clearly.

Weed-Be-Gone

Montgomery Ward - later, Wards - one of the oldest retail stores in America to be transformed to an online shopping site and had been around over 100 years before beginning to lose relevancy and adapting to the retail marketplace. The competition was moving into their market.

Jack Welch of GE Capital, who purchased the majority stock and ownership in Wards in the late 90s and brought Roger Goddu in to operate as President and CEO, Welch informed Goddu, *"You have two years to meet the performance objectives."*

There were numerous initiatives that Roger put into play to meet the deadline. Our company happened to be one of those initiatives to help focus on leadership development for Wards.

Roger opened and closed every one of our leader development sessions with encouraging words to support his executive teams. He shared a story with us during one of those opening statements about a guy outside of Chicago that not only was meeting his performance goal but was surpassing them by a measurable degree.

Roger wanted to recognize and reward this particular manager. He invited the press to meet him at the store. He met all the TV camera crews and reporters in front of the store for a surprise visit. However, as he was walking in the front of the store, Roger noticed weeds throughout the parking lot, some of which were coming up to mid-calf height. Roger asked the TV crews to wait out front for a few minutes while he went in to have a word with the manager first.

He walked in, asked for the manager, and was sent to his office in the back of the store. Roger asked the manager why the weeds were growing in the parking lot much less left to grow up to calf height. The manager made the mistake of replying with what Roger called, something really, really, really foolish.

> *"I did not know the weeds were there. I never enter the store through the front. I always enter from the back."*
>
> Roger replied, *"Are you telling me you do not enter your store through the eyes of your customer?"*

Roger proceeded with the recognition and spotlighted the store's success. But shortly after the event, Roger sent the store manager a case of Weed-Be-Gone along with a note to spend the next few weekends **personally** ensuring that all the weeds were removed. The point is, leaders will celebrate the significant wins, but will also hold others accountable whether it's weeds in the parking lot or falling short of performance targets.

Houston, We Have a Problem

The fifth trigger point that moves Actualizers to their backup pattern, Apollyon, is a major crisis. Gene Kranz, former NASA Flight Director, received the infamous call during the Apollo 13 mission, *"Houston, we've got a problem."* His story clearly illustrates the Actualizer leader moving into the backup Apollyon management style without negativity or meanness but others know that they mean business." On April 13, 1970, two days after the launch of Apollo 13 - the seventh manned Apollo mission flight - Gene Kranz arrived at his office. It was just like any other day until he received the news that an oxygen tank had exploded aboard the spacecraft. The next four days were a series of *"astronauts, engineers, black coffee and cigarettes"* in a combined effort to bring the crew home safely.

> *"The theme for that day was, 'We have never lost an American in space, and we sure as hell aren't going to lose one now,'"* Kranz recalled telling his controllers shortly after the explosion. Though he did not at the time use the famous phrase, *"Failure is not an option,"* popularized by the movie, the feeling was on target. *"This crew is coming home. ... and we will make that happen,"* he told his staff. *"From that moment forward, that team had their directions and they pulled off a miracle over the next four days."* [20]

> *"During the initial moments after the explosion on Apollo 13, Mission Control was working furiously to make sense of what was happening. New failures and alarms were occurring with each moment, and every engineer on duty was desperately trying to make sense of the tide of information."*

[20] Bos, C., Oct 07, 2013. AwesomeStories.com. "Apollo 13 - Gene Kranz at Mission control."

Kranz, as Flight Director, had the responsibility of understanding what his men were telling him and figuring out how to keep the crew safe and the mission on track. He was also tasked with keeping his men focused on their jobs, ensuring that he and his team fulfilled their duties efficiently and correctly. As the astronauts lost oxygen and electrical power for reasons that had yet to be identified, Kranz's voice cut through with a simple command:

> *"Okay now, let's everybody keep cool. Let's solve the problem, but let's not make it any worse by guessing."* [21]

The sense of urgency, decisiveness, and accountability were all present during this unprecedented event. Gene Kranz also demonstrated composure under fire and stayed calm in the midst of a storm, which we believe is one of the utmost qualities of leadership. Like it or not, we transfer a range of emotions in various situations to those who work with us and around us, especially in a crisis or chaotic situation, where we have been blindsided by the unexpected. If we feel panic, pressure, stress, confusion, or anxiety, that is what is transferred to others. But if we exhibit calmness, composure, focus and self-control, those around us will sense that demeanor and emulate the behavior.

Actualizers are 'Mission Control' in organizations balancing the strength of management and the influence of leadership

They offer:

- Poise under pressure
- Tough, smart decision-making
- Added value with their presence
- Help fighting on the front lines with the team
- Leadership demonstrated by being visible and accessible

---

[21] McKay, B. and McKay C., July 20, 2009, A Man's Life, Lessons in Manliness.

- Good judgment with a common sense approach
- Belief in the collective wisdom of the team

Present in the Moment

In contrast to Roger Goddu's Actualizer leadership style where he opened and closed every leadership session visible and present for his teams, we partnered with a communications company for two years on an internal mentoring program whose President exhibited the complete opposite behavior. We worked with the executive team and those who had been identified with potential to move into senior positions at some point in their careers.

- We asked that the company President kick-off the beginning of the year-long program, however, he did not attend.
- We asked that he come to the end of year celebration and personally present certificates of accomplishment. Again, he never stopped by or even acknowledged the request.

The company President continued to be a no-show the entire two years we worked with his most senior-level executive team members. He demonstrated no commitment to, or encouragement of, the next generation of leaders for his organization. He was out of touch with the reality of the impact his presence could make on the team and he added no value to the development process.

Leaders understand they need to be present, but most important, they need to *be there*, or it doesn't count. (Present in the moment)

"The past is great, the future may be great, but never forget to focus on NOW. Embrace now and don't miss it." – **Coach K, Mike Krzyzewski, legendary Basketball coach for Duke University.**

Actualizers are not perfectionists, but they have perfectionist overtones that drive them. They keep raising their own bar, but are never quite satisfied, because even though they hit their bar, they feel they could have done better. They compete against themselves, not against others. They can outperform everyone in the room and somehow still feel disappointment if they miss their own standard of performance. They are not workaholics, but it is the preoccupation with work that can get in the way of being present in the moment and enjoying their own achievements and accomplishments. Actualizers are first to step up and celebrate the success of others and the team but rarely celebrate their own success.

❧

**Ignoring the obvious leads to missed opportunities,
resulting in vanishing options.**

❧

For those who believe you might be an Actualizer, we would like to encourage you to take time to celebrate your own achievements. In addition, be aware that the preoccupation with work may transfer to your personal life as well. Actualizers fully understand the value and importance of balancing work with family. Vacations, weekends, evenings and soccer games are all an integral part of their life. Being physically present isn't the problem. The issue is they are not always fully "there." Actualizers believe they are balancing family and work effectively. However, they tend to remotely monitor work by constantly checking emails, text messages and making business phone calls. This does not go unnoticed by the family. The spouse and children are aware of the lack of attention and quality time and feel they are coming in second to work. It is an unintended consequence of the Actualizer's achiever side. These missed opportunities and vanishing moments of life can lead to the disappointing realization of irretrievable loss and misplaced priorities later in life.

As the great *philosopher* (singer/songwriter) Jimmy Buffet would say, *"If the phone's not ringing it's me."* Unplug from technology and plug into life.

After reviewing all of the leadership patterns, you have most likely attempted to place yourself in one or two behavior styles. If you would like a complete assessment that includes how others also perceive you in the workplace, please contact us to take our 360-degree feedback assessment. LeadAdvantageInc.com

Choices

Place yourself in this situation: you are piloting an airplane with 150 passengers on board. Your aircraft has just stalled out shortly after take-off due to a flock of birds flying into your engines. You only have a moment to decide what you are going to do because you are flying too low and too slow over a densely populated area. You quickly determine you only have three options and none of them good. You know you must risk one of the following three choices.

1. Attempt to continue to fly and land at the next airport
2. Try to turn the plane around and land at the airport from which you came
3. Land in the river

You choose risk 3.

Perhaps in an ideal world, we could live risk-free. The reality is we do not have that luxury, and that's probably a good thing. The world is a better place because those who have gone before us were willing to take risks. Our organizations are better because of the chances others have taken that subsequently led to moving our companies forward.

The ones who are willing to take risks
are the ones who get there first.
Those that get their first, win.

CHAPTER 7

The Boundary Hunters

Our real competitor is not XYZ Company. *The true enemy is often within our own operating environment, settling for the status quo.* In Latin, the status quo means, "the state that we are in." If we can defeat that enemy, remaining viable and relevant will take care of itself.

Challenging the status quo may lead to resistance and criticism, but according to Aristotle, *"There is only one way to avoid criticism: to do nothing, say nothing and be nothing."*

In this fast-changing environment, it is clearly more dangerous to stay the same than it is to change. Successful companies proactively confront issues and implement corrective measures before they become larger and costlier. David Marquet, former submarine captain, and now author, said in, *Turn the Ship Around*, *"A little rudder far from the rocks is better than a lot of rudder close to the rocks."* Does your team monitor issues just "offshore" in time to make corrections, or do they wait until you are already "on the rocks" to react?

> *"If you do not change direction, you may very well end up where you are headed." –* **Lao Tzu, The Father of Taoism**

Our leadership assessment results show that those taking appropriate, moderate to high risks increase the probability of moving more quickly into higher management positions. In general, we have a tendency to risk less when we have something to gain and we risk more when we have something to lose. Think about Las Vegas, for example. As people lose money, they start doubling down on bets trying to win the money back. That's what makes Vegas work. However, when we have won money and are in the black, we tend to place smaller bets.

Similarly, think of your favorite football team. When they have a lead in the game, the tendency is to play it safe and stop taking risks. They play *not to lose,* acting more conservatively rather than continuing to take the chances needed to win. Often, the opposing team catches up to them. The losing team is still taking chances and risking big in order to win the game.

This applies to business as well. When everything seems to be doing well, we tend to maintain the status quo, not willing to take bigger risks with change. We hold on to the money and conventional methods that appear to be working. We stay the course, taking the path of least resistance and only seeing what is easiest to see; what we want to see versus what we need to see.
The enemy within is an illusion of doing well, while we march in place. We are not going anywhere, but the competitor is moving forward without us. If we start losing, we are more apt to take bigger risks to try to turn the situation around.

Those at the higher levels did not get there nor will they stay there by avoiding risks. They got there by being willing to take appropriate risks along the way. However, risk-taking is often viewed as gambling, rolling the dice, all or nothing, Evil Knievel style. The truth is, taking calculated risk can improve performance of a team, department or organization. It is being willing to define and implement the risk after appropriate consideration and planning that makes this approach effective.

✍

Leaders look at risk differently.
Leaders play to win versus play *not to lose*.

✍

Leaders are willing to go against the tide and invest in greater results. Leaders have the courage to make the decision to change and then will involve the team. Leaders will include the team on three key elements to implement any successful change. First, as referenced in Chapter 2, we must address "The Why" or purpose. A leader will pull the team together and communicate clearly about why it is important or necessary to make a change.

Second, an element that is the most thought about but least talked about is informing the team, "what's in it for them." When any significant level of change is about to be implemented, the team wants to know, "What's in it for me (WIIFM)?' If not addressed, it is a potential missed opportunity and can undermine and completely derail success. Realizing the team is unlikely to raise the question, except with one another, a leader will defuse the issue by raising the question and answering it for the team.
The WIIFM should be a combination of both tangible and intangible benefits.

Third, a leader will Empower the Vision by providing a picture of what success looks like. Rick's firm, midway through his 25 years of ownership, chose to raise the stakes and risk to achieve further success. He decided that it was time for the company to go to the next level and continue to play to win. In an offsite location, he met with the entire staff to announce his decision.

> *"Team we are doing great and we are enjoying success, but I believe we now have the potential to join the top leadership companies in the country. Instead of settling for the status quo, let's risk and try to double our business in the next two years."*

He calculated the financial investment required for that lofty objective. If successful, an all-inclusive trip to Jamaica would be included in the reward. He answered "the why" for the team and the purpose of the change. It was the opportunity to join the top tier leadership firms in the country who primarily focused on executive level development. He then addressed how the team could make it happen.

*"We will need to change the way we live and work.
We will need to elevate the way we think. We will
need to sacrifice more in terms of our time, energy
and effort. We will work harder and need to think
differently. We will need to increase our level of
excellence and talent. We will need to give up
individual achievement and the comfort of what
we know for something new for the greater good
of everyone involved."*

Then he addressed what was in it for them. If the team was
successful, they would all be part of something special and be
able to celebrate the experience that together they achieved the
highest level of success. They would have earned the distinction
of acquiring clients from the largest and most successful
companies inside and outside the country (intangibles). If the
team succeeded, the tangible benefits would come as well, such as
higher salaries, new equipment, additional staff, increased perks,
and the additional celebration of an all-inclusive trip to Jamaica.
The tickets were placed in a glass case so that the team would see
it as they arrived each morning and have a visual reminder.

Finally, Rick empowered the vision by creating a picture of
what success would look like. It is critical that the team sees
what you see, wants what you want, and understands success is
both reachable and attainable. If so, they will embrace it, own
it and commit to the vision. Rick's company referred to the
top tier leader development firms as the elite five. These five
companies had the reputation for providing the highest level of
executive leadership development. Rick noticed that all five firms
required the executive clients to travel to their firm or location for
development. Rick said,

*"This is our entry point, our window of opportunity
and our competitive advantage. Their clients must
go to them for development. Our strategy will be
to take the mountain to our clients. We can then
view the world through their eyes, better relate*

to their challenges, and most importantly, we can share in their reality. Have any of you ever had the experience of standing at the peak or near the peak of a mountain and witnessed how the clouds in the sky appear to literally fuse with the top of the mountain? The breath-taking view seems endless. For me, that experience signified that our dreams really are without boundaries and that we are limitless in what we can accomplish together when we are unified and united in our purpose and our belief. We can do this. We will do this!"

There were specific measurements along the way, such as moving the revenue bar higher and gaining specific clients, etc. Rick's company achieved the target in 18 months, not two years, and celebrated in Jamaica ma'n!!!!

This means Leaders take risks and also being willing to challenge the status quo if necessary and go a different direction.

Unlike the majority of companies who try to cut and slash their way through a financial downturn and difficult times, legendary leaders understand that risk and change must occur, or we become stagnant, weak and may lose our best talent. We are not talking revolutionary changes that include high-stakes gambling or survival instinct but taking appropriate risk to move the organization forward.

We all take risks every day in our personal and professional lives. For example, we risk in relationships with others. We risk in our jobs with the decisions we make daily and weekly. Most of the time, we risk by choice. We risk in an effort to make something better versus settling for something less. Sometimes we risk without having a choice, like Captain Sullenberger from the beginning of the chapter, who landed a plane on the Hudson River. He found himself in a crisis situation with a short amount of time to find a resolution. With boldness and courage,

Captain Sullenberger took a calculated risked and won big—all passengers walked away.

∝

Whatever the reason or circumstance, risk is part of our life and part of our job. It is part of what defines a legendary leader and leads to great teams and companies.

∝

American Family Life Assurance Company were challenged with brand awareness in the United States. However, they were the number one selling insurance company in Japan. The CEO, Dan Amos, hired a marketing group to develop a new slogan and ad campaign to help promote brand recognition. The marketing agency decided to call the company by its acronym to shorten the name as they were tossing around ideas for a campaign— AFLAC.

During one internal meeting, a marketing manager asked, *"What is the name of that company we are pitching?"*

Someone in the group remarked, *"It's AFLAC, AFLAC, AFLAC!"*

Everyone laughed and said it sounded like a duck quacking. An idea was born. They took a risk and presented the idea to the CEO.

Dan Amos liked the idea. He stopped them in the middle of their presentation and said, *"There's the future of our company."*

He was willing to take a risk that made sense for the company, it paid off, and the rest is history!

Risk, Risky or Reluctant

Each of the management and leadership patterns discussed in previous chapters have a different comfort level with risk and change.

The Apollyon and the Strategist patterns are high risk-takers. Apollyons roll the dice high and take reactive risks with their own ideas without seeking input from others. This can lead to high-cost, reckless and risky actions.

The Strategist, also a high risk-taker, will listen to input and then take the time to persuade others to embrace their viewpoint and their high risk, high reward idea. Since the Strategist plan is known to lack details and substance, they may try to spin their way to success by throwing additional money at an idea to achieve the level of success they have envisioned. The ideas keep expanding and becoming more and more grandiose and risky.

> *"He is a spellbinding spinner of visions and his biggest strength is his ability to mesmerize even the most savvy people with sales pitches for new, but sometimes flawed, products... because the details are often left behind."* - **A quote about Stephen Jobs in the 1993 Wall Street Journal**.

The Sentinel, or Godfather, will take moderate, calculated risks as long as they are based on conventional and traditional methods that follow *"the way we've always done things."* When working for a Sentinel, they are less likely to support and encourage us to think outside the boundaries. They prefer the customary tried-and-true ways of getting things done.

The Actualizer also takes calculated informed risks, encouraging input from others and exploring unique avenues and ideas, but they always bring it back appropriately to what makes sense at a realistic level while offering the best benefit to the team or organization.

The Synergist and Criterion patterns are conservative or low risk-takers and will traditionally resist change. The Synergists are uncomfortable with change because they need consensus to move forward. Typically, with risk and change, there will not be a consensus. Criterions will dig their heels in and challenge change because they prefer the conformity and the status quo. They know what they like and like what they know. Change is not what they know and is not comfortable. It causes them to lose a sense of security. Synergists and Criterions often experience limitations in moving higher in the organization due to this lack of risk-taking acumen.

The best way to minimize the resistance of Synergists or Criterions is to include them in the change process. The more input they can provide and the more involved they are in the change, the more likely they are to maintain their sense of security and embrace the change. Criterion become active participants in the change process. Over time, the new process or new way of doing something will become more natural.

Boundaries of Change

"If you don't like how things are, change it! You're not a tree." – **Jim Rohn, Business Entrepreneur**

Change involves risk. As we said earlier, we have a tendency to complicate behavior. We also have a propensity to complicate the element of change and as a result, are often fearful of it. We are fearful of the unknown, but by giving change a name in terms of identity and definition, the fear begins to fade, and we are better able to confront the challenge. Leaders will simplify. So, let's simplify the dynamic of change. All change, regardless of business or industry, gravitates toward being either Maintenance, Developmental, Transitional, or Transformational.

Routine decisions require **Maintenance Change,** *doing the same things*, which only include repairing, fixing or preventing in order to maintain the status quo, similar to maintaining a car when the battery dies, or tires need to be changed. It is doing the minimum to get by. This is important for any organization to keep the engine running smoothly and ensure continued operation, however, maintenance is not a measurement of success.

In today's environment, a company cannot survive and remain viable, competitive and relevant long-term by only relying on Maintenance Change. It would be like having a football team with only one play in the playbook and calling the same run over and over again. How's that strategy going to work out? The opponent will crush you. There is little or no risk in the Maintenance phase and very little reward, other than they can continue to safely drive the car. Most Criterions and Synergists fall into this category of Maintenance Change; minor evolution, definitely not revolution.

Enhancing, improving, and building upon what is already in place is referred to as **Developmental Change**. It is basically *improving the things we are already doing*. An example would include hotel chains, which have added free Wi-Fi access, complimentary breakfasts, evening cocktails, business centers, and workout facilities in an effort to create customer loyalty by adding improved conveniences for guests. We have added some level of reasonable risk at this point for a reasonable return. It is not expecting explosive growth in the organization, but rather staying competitive with the expectations of the market.

Sentinels and Actualizers are comfortable with this level of change and are always exploring ways to make things better; not following the leader but being the leader. The reward comes in the form of continually being out front of the competition by initiating and implementing these changes in order to gain the greatest returns. By the time the competition replicates the change, the Sentinels and Actualizers have already moved on to the next improvement.

Transitional Change involves *doing things differently* to create, invent or switch something, but has direct links to the past so there is a known outcome. An example would be transitioning from owning an executive limo service to owning an executive flight company. It involves doing things differently, but the company is still providing a form of transportation. At this level of change, risk increases, and rewards are greater. It's all about elevating the company to a higher level. The way business is conducted is elevated, the attitude of both management and employee is elevated, communication with the customer is improved, service is expanded, standards are raised, and prestige is enhanced.

Actualizers will engage comfortably in Transitional change. Apollyons and Strategists are also comfortable with this type of change.

Transformational Change is rebuilding, reframing, redesigning, or recreating, and *doing different things*. With Transformational Change, there is no link to the past and there is generally an unknown outcome. Traditionally, Transformational change was reactive and implemented only as a means of survival - an option of last resort if you will. In this context, it was not about improving but reinventing the company in order to survive in the long-term…and reinventing is not about changing the current state but instead about creating "what doesn't yet exist." It was transforming the organization into a totally different creation. For example, Nokia was originally a merged paper mill, rubber works, and cable works company. Now they are known for mobile phones and mobile games.

Interestingly, companies today are also using transformational change to produce an additional source of income to diversify in a totally unrelated field. We are seeing a more proactive move toward Transformational change. An example would be Google, an online search engine, who began creating driverless cars—a completely different focus. Also, Panasonic radically restructured its core electronics business and expanded into areas such as agriculture and electric car batteries.

Both Maintenance and Developmental Change can typically be implemented without too much time, effort or money. Empowered employees should be able to adequately handle change at this level. Transitional and Transformational Change require certain guiding principles.

Guiding Principles for Successful Change

Choose Wisely Between Old Patterns and Winning Formulas:

"Although we have the technological capability to accomplish almost anything, do we have the corresponding wisdom to know the things we should change?" - **Lee Iaccoca, former Executive of Ford Motor Company and Chrysler Corporation.**

When making choices regarding changes, it is critical that we do not tamper with winning formulas. Know what brought the organization to life.

What brought Coke to life was the original Coke formula. It was such a sacred formula, it is still said to be guarded in a safe in Atlanta today. In 1985, Coke decided they would introduce "New Coke" to replace the Classic Coke and the original formula as a means of re-energizing the cola market.

"On that day, The Coca-Cola Company took arguably the biggest risk in consumer goods history, announcing that it was changing the formula for the world's most popular soft drink, and spawning consumer angst the likes of which no business has ever seen. Robert Goizueta, Chairman and Chief Executive Officer of Coca-Cola Company in 1985 received a letter addressed to *"Chief Dodo, The Coca-Cola Company."* (He often said he was more upset that it was actually delivered to him!) Another person wrote to him asking for his autograph because, in years to come, the signature of '*one of the dumbest executives in American business history' would be worth a fortune.*" [22]

Coke brought back the original formula, Classic Coke, less than three months later due to the tremendous outcry from consumers who were devoted to the original coke and did not like the unfamiliar sweeter version of New Coke.

They were stockpiling cases of Classic Coke in their basements and calling and sending letters by the droves in protest of the change. This Coke fiasco is an iconic example of a company that obviously chose unwisely because they failed to factor in the magnitude of their loyalty base and violated what brought them to life—their sacred winning formula.

Prepare for Knowns and Unknowns:

Decisions need to be made by the leader and the team regarding how to maneuver around the obstacles; those known and unknowns mentioned earlier. As discussed in Chapter 1, the knowns refer to those obstacles we have knowledge of and we can move forward with a plan to correct or mitigate.

Tom Skains, mentioned earlier, had a plan for mitigating an internally competitive environment. He had previously worked for an organization that had a destructive, highly competitive operating environment that created division within the company. He understood how counter-productive this behavior could be to an organization, so when he was selected as CEO of Piedmont Natural Gas, he wanted to ensure that a silo mentality did not create the same divisive situation.

He made the decision to rotate management positions to lead different areas of responsibility every few years. These

---

[22] The Real Story of New Coke, By: Conversations Staff, 2012. http://www.coca-colacompany.com/stories/coke-lore-new-coke

reassignments removed barriers, created unity and eliminated silos. Additionally, the moves generated a higher level of energy internally where promotions, learning and growth in their careers, and the development of bench strength for the organization became paramount. Therefore, in the event an essential player left, someone else was prepared to step in seamlessly.

The unknowns, on the other hand, are gaps in our knowledge that we need to research and uncover. Going through worst-case scenarios and discussing "what if" situations or the potential knockout punch can help alleviate some of the unknowns.

A colleague and friend, Jim Little, Executive Consultant for Nuclear Energy Programs, is a huge advocate of forward thinking and looking at an issue from a different perspective in order to find better solutions. One method he encourages using is inversion:

> *"This way of thinking, in which you consider the opposite of what you want, is known as inversion... As I have studied it more, I have begun to realize that inversion is a rare and crucial skill that nearly all great thinkers use to their advantage."*
> - **James Clear**

A hurricane task force goes through a repetitive and exacting exercise so if a hurricane hits land, they are prepared to handle maintaining lines of communication, have an evacuation plan, and a process to rescue those who are stranded or in need of medical assistance. There is not a lot of time to respond. They need to be prepared to make decisions by anticipating any negative outcomes and have a plan of action to respond quickly.

Coke created a "hurricane" when it did not anticipate the public's reaction to changing its original formula to "New Coke." This could have been a potential knock-out punch and extremely detrimental to them. Perhaps they did not conduct sufficient market taste tests or test the right audience. The decision cost the company a lot of money in a short amount of time before they figured out how to return to it's winning formula.

Have an Exit Strategy:

Remember that HOPE is not a strategy. Sometimes what appears to be the most viable path or the quickest path may not be the path that will take us to ultimate victory. The last thing we need to do when headed in the wrong direction is get there quicker. Like a chess game, we want to anticipate the next move of our competitors and adjust our strategy accordingly or change it completely. Hopefully, we won't need one, but if we do, have an Exit Strategy with a clearly defined set of criteria for when to activate the plan.

Google's view on Exit Strategy is "earlier exits over early exits." In other words, if you're not early, you're late.

At this level of higher-risk, higher-reward change, the tendency is to delay making the hard call and to continue to throw good money after bad, primarily due to the political implications and the ensuing consequences of accountability.

During the 2008 and 2009 financial collapse, a close friend and wealth management advisor said that he had three types of clients:

- those who had sound reason to believe they could weather the crisis
- those who had no reason to believe they could weather the crisis and triggered their exit strategy in time to live and fight another day, and finally
- his ill-fated clients who had already failed but did not know it yet. Their destiny sealed, but they were still rearranging the deck chairs on the Titanic.

ॐ

Stay the course or cut our losses? Leaders make the call.

ॐ

As Miami Herald columnist, Leonard Pitts, said regarding the future, which involves risk-taking and change,

> *"For every man or woman who seems able to see around corners, there's a million others walking into walls, their vision of what will be hopelessly clouded by what they want and by what is. We tend to see the future as an extreme version of the present, rather than as something that exists on its own."*

Purposeful

David A. Wright is an American businessman, politician, energy policy advisor, and nominated by President Donald Trump to the Nuclear Regulatory Commission.

We asked David Wright in an interview to tell us a defining moment in his life. Something that transcended organizations and positions and changed his viewpoint or impacted his philosophical perspective that he has been able to use and apply throughout his career.

His answer was quick: surviving colon cancer. A year later, his twenty-seven-year-old daughter also had colon cancer and survived.

> He said, *"When you go through something like that, you learn about what makes you tick and what is important. It helps re-focus or focus on what is important in every application in life, how you treat others, how to approach work, etc. You have a choice to be better or to be sad, to fight or not, to be positive or negative. There is no gray area, you have to decide. After recovery, I decided to do things different[sic] and better, such as serving. I realized you can't sit on the sidelines, you have to make a difference. The leadership application was that I realized I had been successful, but not purposeful and not fulfilled. Now I am unafraid and confident and serve for a different purpose."*

CHAPTER 8

Intentional Focus or Unintentional Consequences

Over the years of working with top executives in fortune 500 companies, we have had the opportunity of asking them what they consider to be the top leadership qualities that they look for in their executives and management teams (some of which are incorporated throughout this book). The list is long. However, after observing some of these same executives over time and tracking their careers, and then comparing them to other truly great leaders we have worked with, we have come to realize that many do not actually practice these qualities and often fail to take the appropriate initiative to develop and cultivate those leadership qualities within their own culture. If these executives are not living these qualities themselves or bringing them to life and demonstrating them within their own organization, one can only conclude they are willing to settle for being just like the rest versus being better than the rest.

We have also worked with many exceptional leaders over the years and gleaned numerous insights and examples from them. Their shared insights have been enormously beneficial and have allowed us to be continual learners and purposeful about our own leadership practices.

We have often been asked about our views on top leadership qualities and have compiled our own "Top 10" list of Leadership traits which we cover fully in our sessions. Since this is our final chapter, we would like to conclude by sharing some "thoughts at large" about that mystical force we call Leadership, which encompass some of those top leadership traits and qualities.

We also may debunk some leadership misconceptions along the way. Importantly, owning, living and practicing the following observations all require an intentional focus and if embraced will lead to traits of truly legendary leaders. Perhaps you may find a nugget or two, or perhaps, you may find some controversy. Either way, we hope to make you think. The truth is, if we make one another think, we add value.

"The Desk is a Dangerous Place from Which to View the World."

John Le Carre

There are two lines of communication in every organization, the Formal and the Informal. Which is the purest and most reliable line of communication? Of course, it's the Informal. Who has clear access to the Informal? The employees. Radio silence for all others . . . except for those exclusive and trusted few managers/leaders who have earned the right to be included in the conversations and being informed of what is really going on in the trenches. The only path to inclusion, and not always guaranteed, leave the desk and regularly visit the Front Lines where reality takes place every day. Eat and talk with the troops. Ask about what's working, what's not and *"how can I fix it?"* Leaders listen. And then do it . . . in a timely manner! They also pitch in and add value. Leaders get their hands dirty.

This is not about a "cameo" appearance or a photo op session. This is personal and private. This is about being visible and accessible to the employees even if no one else knows about it, staying awhile, and learning something. Leaders tap into reality and the employee's view of the world, as they know it.

Employees and colleagues need to know that they matter and that they are a valuable asset to the organization and team. This can only happen through a mutual trust and respect. If I trust you, I am more willing to share my concerns, ideas or thoughts with you. If I respect you, I am more willing to have your back and go the extra mile. Being visible and accessible is the best way to build trust and respect. Leave the desk, walk around, observe, and connect!

On one of our recent client visits in Florida, as we were checking into the hotel, we experienced something, or rather did not experience something, that truly captured the meaning of the phrase, "leaders get their hands dirty."

There were three check-in lines and three to four people standing in each line. A few minutes later a tour bus pulled up in front of the hotel. Now each line increased to 10-12 people deep with customers waiting to register and check into their room. A manager opened the door from behind the front desk and noticed the long lines. He was not in a uniform, but in a suit with his nametag on the suit pocket, clearly identifying him as a manager versus a uniformed employee. About that time, we caught his eye. We assumed he was stepping out to help speed up the check-in process. But, he smiled quickly and said, *"Someone will be right with you. Thank you for your patience."* Then he quickly stepped back into the office and closed the door.

It reminded us of calling a doctor's office and getting the dreaded recording that says, *"Your business is important to us. A representative will be right with you. Thank you for your patience."* Yet, you have probably already been on hold several minutes and begun thinking, *"if my business was that important to you, you would find a way to answer my call quicker. Not to mention, my patience ran out 5 minutes ago."*

The hotel manager gave us the same impression. If our business was important to you, why did you not step out on the front lines and pitch in? What a wasted opportunity for that manager to roll up his sleeves and get his hands dirty and add value with his presence. He could have sped up the process by helping the agent with room keys, answering questions, calling the bellman, or escorting people to the elevator. The list of ways he could have added value is a long one and the only way he does not add value…is by doing nothing and shutting the door! If we do not add value even in small ways, can we be trusted to add value in larger ways? Probably not.

Most of those in line likely did not even notice the manager looking from behind the door. However, **all** of them would have noticed him coming out and pitching in.

Ethical Choices and Individual Voices
Roger Boisjoly

"If you see something wrong, and you do not stop it, whether you had anything to do with it or not, you are responsible for the outcome."
- Del Yocam, former Executive VP at Apple

This is the view of the world of an Actualizer where profit and character are equally factored into their choices.

Robert Carothers, University of Rhode Island president had to make such a call when 31 members of the football team decided to circle a fraternity house after they had been denied into the fraternity party the prior weekend. Six of the players entered the house and beat up several of the fraternity brothers. Robert Carothers was so upset about the conduct of the team that he suspended the six players who beat up the students. He also suspended the other 25 players who surrounded the house, and then the entire remainder of the team - all 72 players - for the homecoming game against the University of Connecticut that weekend because they knew about the incident and did nothing to stop it.

Carothers had to decide to do the right thing despite the criticism from the players and their families, the faculty and the community who were all angry with him. Carothers said, *"if members of a team couldn't adhere to acceptable standards of behavior, then for one weekend, there would no longer be a team."*

In addition, the University of Connecticut was outraged, claiming the forfeit cost the school at least $150,000 in gate receipts. To which Carothers responded, *"Send me the bill. This is not about football. This is about community standards. This is about character."*

Every fall, Carothers addressed the university's incoming freshman. *"I tell them that by the time they walk across that quadrangle in four years for graduation, they should have some clarity about what they stand for, and what they won't stand for."*[23]

Leadership and ethical behavior are inseparable.

There are no Guilty People in Prison

Hiring and retaining qualified, high-performing individuals who will contribute to the overall success of the organization is vital. Often left out, but just as vital, is acknowledging and being intolerant of habitual poor performers. *"There really are guilty people in prison."*

Many Human Resource managers naturally gravitate toward Criterion behavior, which can fall into paralysis-analysis, or Synergist behavior, emphasizing people over tasks.

---

[23] Plaschke, B. 1996. University Chief Benches Football Team as a Lesson, http://articles. latimes.com/1996-10-26/news/mn-58029_1_team-university-football

Unfortunately, extended prolonged patience with poor performers ends up creating unintended consequences for the organization. To Human Resource's credit, they do provide a "safe harbor" environment for employees, which is a good thing, but when it becomes over-protecting the guilty, the bar of performance is lowered for everyone in the company and creates an attitude of apathy that begins to permeate throughout the operating environment. Is your organization becoming so consumed by the prospect of letting poor performers go free that you miss the obvious, the cost to the Company in terms money, time, morale, and achievement?

General Powell during a briefing to the Outreach to America Program where he provided lessons in Leadership explains,

> *"Good leadership involves responsibility to the welfare of the group, which means that some people will get angry at your actions and decisions. It's inevitable - if you're honorable. Trying to get everyone to like you is a sign of mediocrity. You'll avoid the tough decisions, you'll avoid confronting the people who need to be confronted, and you'll avoid offering differential rewards based on differential performance because some people might get upset. Ironically, by procrastinating on the difficult choices, by trying not to get anyone mad, and by treating everyone equally "nicely" regardless of their contributions, you'll simply ensure that the only people you'll wind up angering are the most creative and productive people in the organization."*

Barking Dogs Don't Chase Parked Cars

unknown

If the dogs are silent, worry.
If the dogs are barking, sleep well.
You've done your job!

Tough measures, implementing changes and hard choices are part of proactively moving our companies forward or preventing challenging times. However, when we do this - make tough choices and initiate change - there will be resistance, the dogs are going to bark. The reality is, tough calls, by their very nature can be painful. If all decisions were simply black or white, right or wrong, and just not a problem for most of us, it would be an easy call. The tough calls, however, are more often between right and right, or tough and tougher, with perhaps only a matter of degrees separating the two choices. After more deliberation, re-thinking the options and the consequences, it is commitment time. Leaders do what they know they have to do, they make the call and then they own it. However, the one making the decision certainly understands their decision is not likely to please everyone and can create a backlash of criticism.

> *"I do not seek unpopularity as a badge of honor, but sometimes it is the price of leadership and the cost of conviction."* - **Tony Blair, Former Prime Minister of the UK**

Tough calls are not always popular but necessary to the success of the organization. Realizing that tough is not mean and that as long as integrity is part of the decision and you believe it is the right choice, then move forward and take action.

> *"Being responsible sometimes means pissing people off."*
> - **General Colin Powell**.

It is interesting to note that this was Colin Powell's number one lesson in leadership.

Take That Hill

"A young man fell asleep during math class. He woke up as the bell rang, looked up at the blackboard, and copied the two problems that were there. He assumed they were the homework for the night. He went home and labored the rest of the afternoon and into the evening knowing if he didn't complete his homework, he would surely fail the class. He couldn't figure out either one, but he kept trying for the rest of the week. Finally, he got the answer to one and brought it to the class. The teacher was absolutely stunned. The boy feared he had done too little too late. It turned out the problem he solved was supposedly unsolvable."

"How did he do it? He was able to do what was thought to be impossible because he believed it was possible. He not only believed it was possible, he believed that if he didn't solve it he would fail the class. Had he known the problem was unsolvable he could never have done it." - Think and Grow Rich for Coaches – **Napoleon Hill and Will Craig**

Sometimes leaders must *Take that Hill* against all odds and do what others think is impossible. Leaders find a way! Leaders can also motivate the team to take on the challenge. This is not ropes and ladders and simply developing trust, although trust is certainly part of it. This is about believing **we as a team** can do something remarkable, something greater than ourselves. It is about inspiring others to follow us even into the abyss.

US Navy Lieutenant Commander, Dudley "Mush" Morton's feisty and daring nature led him to command the Navy's most fierce warships of all time, the USS Wahoo. Former Wahoo sailor, Chief Yeoman Forrest Sterling said,

> *"When I first met Commander Morton it only took me one minute to realize that I would follow that man to the bottom of the ocean if necessary. Mush was a true leader of men and knew his business inside and out."*[24]

Real Value or Just an Illusion

Committees have little or no value in the real world. Just ask Washington! They are primarily opportunities for Committee members to push their own agenda. There is an absence of decisiveness and individual accountability, and by giving the "illusion of progress," and creating a lot of chatter, committees are provided "ground cover noise," justification for the inordinate amount of time spent on reaching NO conclusion. The meetings usually then adjourn with someone suggesting, *"I propose that we have another meeting."* REALLY?

If we can agree that our success is ultimately measured in terms of "Money and Time," any measured value of a committee's success can be clearly offset or exceeded by the value of lost time.

---

[24] Entrepreneur Magazine, 2011. 10 Lessons from American Military Leaders, https://www.entrepreneur.com/slideshow/220667

One obvious solution is to move from a Committee-driven process to a team-driven process. Selectively choose a 4 to 6-member team (ideal decision-making number of people), appoint the appropriate Leader (empowered with authority) and set a specific timeline along with clearly defined objectives and expectations.

Tap into the collective wisdom of the team, challenge one another, debate the issues, explore outside the lines of conventional methods...and when the designated timeline is up, take decisive action.

> *"You can use the fanciest computers to gather the numbers, run those numbers through countless meetings, attended by countless numbers of people; but in the end, you have to set a timetable and act."* - **Lee Iacocca**

When does an unproductive process become the master of our time? There is a myriad of subjects that fall under this area of becoming masters of our time. Time is a measurement of success and meetings tend to be the biggest time waster of all. However, meetings are part of our reality so how do we streamline unproductive meetings into time well spent? A few years ago, we were working with a senior leadership team from a Southwest manufacturing firm. After providing the Senior Management Team with a proven method and format (Blueprint) for conducting more efficient meetings, and how to use it in their strategic planning process, the president asked if he could have the floor for a moment.

He then said to his team,

> *"This piece alone is worth the cost of the program and the time we have invested here. We consume so much of our time in meetings and at a cost, quite frankly, I don't like to think about. We are going to implement this idea immediately."*

Inefficient and Unproductive Meetings Cost Both Time and Money and Hinder Performance *25

Treasure Hunting

"Growth and comfort do not coexist."
- Ginni Rommety, CEO of IBM

Perhaps the single most important attribute that Abraham Lincoln possessed was his ability to challenge himself to continually learn. He was passionate about self-improvement. And he didn't stop learning when he moved into the White House. Lincoln went to work every day with the attitude of a learner, and the result was that he continued to improve his leadership skills. The times demanded that he be good, and he made himself great.[26]

What if you:

- Failed in high school (almost every course, even receiving a zero in physics)

- Submitted drawings to your school yearbook, but were rejected

- Failed in college (again, almost every course)

- Failed at golf

- Failed socially

- Failed at dating (proposed marriage to your girlfriend, but were rejected)

---

[25] This Strategic Planning Process format is included as one of our Seven Deadly Sins of **Mis-**Management in one of our leadership programs.

[26] Davis, K. 2016. Five Presidential Attributes Every Sales Manager Needs, https://toplineleadership.com/five-presidential-attributes-every-sales-manager-needs/

- Had your work rejected by two well-renowned news papers
- Applied to Disney as an Animator, but were rejected

How many of us would have just given up?

Charles Schulz, best known for his Peanuts comic strips, experienced all of these, one failure after another, but never gave up.

If you see potential in yourself, even though you think no one else does, let us encourage you to step up and create your own destiny. When we tap into our potential where there appears to be nothing to tap into, you become even a stronger leader, against all odds. Sometimes a lack of confidence, prior disappointments or previous failures may cause us to be reluctant at putting ourselves at any further risk, exposure or rejection. But, if we can find the inner strength to persevere and tap into our belief of our own potential, the reluctant leader may just discover the treasure of becoming a great leader.

Leaders learn from failure.

Focus on the Target, Not the Distraction

A well-known golf professional was recently in search of a new caddy. He narrowed it down to two choices. As a final interview, he scheduled playing a round of golf with each of them. He had already been out with the first candidate and was now playing a round with the second candidate. On a particularly challenging hole, he turned to the candidate and asked, *"What do you think I should do?"*

The caddy responded, *"Well, you need to be aware that to the left of the green is a water hazard."* The caddy went into detail on the hazard and the approximate distance from the green.

The pro stopped the caddy and said, *"Don't tell me where the problem is, I do not want to focus on the hazard, I want to focus on the target...the flag. I do not need to be distracted by the problem."* The pro knew immediately he would go with candidate number one whose only focus was achieving the goal.

Leaders are aware of the distractions and the noise around them, but they will not allow the distraction to override the task at hand. They want to be **on time** and **on point** with *solutions,* not excuses.

A Collection of Habits

"I can't change the direction of the wind, but I can adjust my sails to always reach my destination."
– **Jimmy Dean**

Whether we are talking about risk, change, problem-solving, decision-making, or relationships at work, it all comes from one source: behavior. Early in life, we develop habits. It's a collection of those habits that shape and form our behavior. We all develop a set of good habits or traits and we all have a set of bad habits or flaws. Like a New Year's Resolution, most of us are aware, or we are made aware, of our bad habits, and for improvement purposes, we make an oath to ourselves that we will change for the better. Sounds good at the time, but like that New Year's Resolution, we often end up defaulting back to our old ways...AGAIN.

For example, when playing golf, we use methods (our swing, stance, grip) in ways that feel natural to us, even though they may be wrong. As our golf game continues to drive us totally insane, we decide to take a golf lesson. The pro shows us how to change and improve our grip or swing. We become excited during the lesson, tell ourselves we can do this, and how great it is going to be to "*beat-the-hell out of our buddies during our regular weekly golf game.*" However, when we return to the course to play a game, the grip and swing the pro taught us feels uncomfortable and our tendency is to go back to what feels natural. Obviously, it takes time and practice to develop a new habit and have it become more natural to us.

The **patterns of behavior**, which we discussed throughout the book, are the centerpiece of our Leader Development process. Participants receive an in-depth analysis and review of their individual pattern of behavior. We frequently hear from participants that, "*I am different at work than at home*" inferring that their behavior is "*better*" at home than at work or vice versa. The truth is that we are pretty much the same at both home and work, but our behavior is simply magnified at one or the other. The good, the bad, and the ugly. Just ask your spouse!

The good news though is that we can change our behavior, once we know what to change. We all want to change and grow as leaders, but sometimes we do not know where to begin. Our process provides those starting points for participants to help them make sustainable habit changes.

Our pattern can never be an excuse for our behavior.

If you would like to receive a reality check and know where your colleagues have placed you in these behavior patterns, please contact us. www.leadadvantageinc.com

Leaders are Committed, Convicted and Courageous

Comments like leadership being a "soft skill" are one of those really, really, really foolish things people say that will infuriate a leader. Using leadership and soft skills in the same sentence makes about as much sense as fish needing umbrellas. Leadership is the toughest aspect of management. Management is a task, an order or an objective. But when you have to weigh in the responsibility to plan, organize, strategize and accept the realities - the price to be paid for taking the hill in terms of the casualty count, potential criticism, accountability - that is the agonizing toughness of leadership.

Air Force Captain Scott O'Grady was shot down over Bosnia in 1995 after flying over hostile territory without authorization in order to take pictures and confirm to the world the massacres that were taking place. The 29-year-old pilot had been missing in Serbia for five days with meager rations of food and water. O'Grady slept by day, covering himself with camouflage netting, and moved only between midnight and 4 a.m. Armed Serbs were never far away, and he often heard gunfire.

Scott O'Grady risked his own life to prove to the world that the Serbs were executing massive numbers of people within their own country. The world was not paying attention to what was happening in Serbia until O'Grady proved the mass bloodshed. The rest of the world then united to stop the killing. Scott O'Grady was committed, convicted and courageous. He was willing to put his own life at risk in order to save people he did not even know by being their voice of truth and freedom.

Soft skill? We beg to differ! **Manager** is a *position title* simply **given** to us by the organization. How many of us have ever heard, "*I aspire to be a Manager?*"

No. We aspire to be leaders. The strength of leadership is a rare and powerful force. Only the few **earn** the Medal of Leadership, and often they earn it behind the curtain versus in the spotlight. Being committed, convicted and courageous transcends our job. It is about belief in a greater purpose.

If an organization is looking for "soft skill" Leadership Development, LeadAdvantage will respectively decline; however, if you want to develop leaders **to think, to work and to take away something real,** we will be honored to accept your invitation.

Remember, discovery always begins with the search. LEADERSHIP, VISION, and PURPOSE are a continuous journey without a final destination. Growth is an endless opportunity. Remain curious, continue to explore outside the boundaries, remove all self-imposed limitations, take appropriate risks with your potential, and most importantly, enjoy the ride.

> *"Achieving your vision doesn't mean you've reached the end of the line. It simply means that you have come to a new starting place."* – **Nido R. Qubein, International speaker, President High Point University**

You, our readers, were the inspiration for writing this book. THANK YOU for allowing us to share our views on what we believe to be the most powerful force available to us (other than a kneel and a prayer). The good news is it's not complicated. It's simply choosing and investing in how we want to live, work, and lead.

Please contact us at www.leadadvantageinc.com
See sample customized program agendas in the back of the book.

Sample Agendas

The Strength of Management, The Influence of Leadership

Participants will learn how to become more productive individuals, contributing to work teams and bottom-line results.

LeadAdvantage uses validated assessments, business simulations, and case studies to initiate self-development efforts by participants. These methods help them to recognize professional and personal behavior patterns so that they can strengthen behaviors that enhance communication and performance.

DAY 1:
CONSENSUS BUILDING FOR
EFFECTIVE DECISION MAKING

Participants engage in a dynamic and highly interactive activity to develop an understanding of how:

- Collaboration improves the quality of decisions, encourages diverse thinking and builds trust and mutual respect within the team
- Projects and tasks can be achieved with a higher level of predictable success by incorporating a "blueprint" for results

Leveraging Your Team
Utilizing your greatest asset – the team – to build unity and achieve results.
Wheel of Success (Part 1)
Faced with a demanding task, teams must work together to achieve results, with time management and communication crucial to success.

Building Successful Board Meetings (Part 2)
Participants will address and discuss how the opposing forces of communication and interpretation can frustrate team effort during any planning and implementation strategy.

Reducing Blindspots in Communication

Participants will be provided a framework for strengthening communication with employees, colleagues and managers, as well as, methods and techniques for improving the quality of information exchanged and shared with others. Skills developed:

- Communication that maximizes productivity and effectiveness
- The ability to adapt communication to different patterns of behavior
- What communication reveals...and what it doesn't

Patterns of Behavior; Impact and Influence

Participants will be provided an in-depth study and profile of the seven management and leadership patterns of behavior. Participants will understand how to:

- Identify each pattern, including strengths and weaknesses, motivations and traits
- Develop a more productive and effective working relationship with others
- Strengthen communication
- Resolve conflict and achieve win-win resolutions
- Match individual styles with compatible roles and responsibilities to improve performance

DAY 2:
BALANCING AND MANAGING PRIORITIES

Balancing individual, team and company priorities can be challenging and difficult. Participants work as a team to confront a task that requires the completion of both an individual and team goal. Participants will address:

- The benefits of trade-offs associated with individual achievement versus company success
- Working under project deadlines and other work-related pressures

Case Study in Leadership and Management

Participants will recognize how different management styles can benefit or disrupt an organization. Divided teams follow a structured format to identify and address managerial issues. During the discussion and facilitation, participants reflect on how to recognize and respond to these types of issues and challenges, and also how their style of management may impact and affect others.

Leadership Pattern Assessment (LPA) Results

Participants will be provided confidential results on their individual behavioral style (surveys completed prior to the session by each participant and their associates). This feedback will include both their primary, as well as their backup style (that which we move to when under pressure or more adverse conditions). Participants will also review and analyze their leadership pattern in ten areas of management, such as:

- Responding to a crisis
- Handling conflict
- Feedback
- Awareness of others

Improving the Probability of Success

Establish a winning formula for self-development based on the LPA results and then implementing realistic action plans and objectives that impact achievement.

Wei Chi: Where Danger Meets Opportunity

This two-day program focuses on the manager's ability to adapt to a constantly changing environment and solve problems in a dynamic, fast-moving workplace. Participants have the opportunity to be assessed on the Leadership Pattern Assessment 360 from The Leadership Advantage program to measure progress toward goals and/or to receive feedback on a Leadership Effectiveness Profile, which examines behavior in specific management situations. The 360-degree metric provides a benchmark to track an employee's development in the workplace. It is recommended that re-assessment take place six months to a year after Program One.

DAY 1:
PARTICIPANT INTRODUCTIONS
INTENTIONAL FOCUS

The program opens with an exercise that explores *actual* versus *ideal* usage of time and priorities and how routine habits and actions can consume our focus and attention. Participants will examine how to re-direct both energy and effort in order to minimize distractions and achieve optimal results.

Beyond the Boundaries
Participants will engage in a dynamic discussion regarding the ultimate challenge confronting organizations today - although we have the technological capability to do almost anything, how do we develop the corresponding ability to choose wisely which things should be done.

Decision Styles Profile
An enlightening management assessment tool that leads to the development of improved decision-making skills. It evaluates the appropriateness with which respondents include others in the decision-making process and the extent to which respondents consider five critical Decision Factors in their decision processes.

Change Orientation Inventory

Participants complete a short self-assessment instrument that measures their ability to both adapt to change as well as innovate and implement new ideas within the organization.

Managing the "Culprits"

- Managing the obstacles that undermine team success
- Overcoming team dysfunctions to achieve optimal results

Building the Foundation for Change

In this discussion, participants will identify the four types of change and how the risks and rewards in each level impact and influence the operating environment. Participants will recognize how communication and implementation strategies can minimize resistance to change and move the organization through transition to genuine commitment.

Carter Racing: - The Impact of Management Decisions

A case study addressing how different types of management can both help and hinder an organization. Teams will collectively analyze the case to determine how to improve communication, planning and making decisions as a team.

DAY 2:
APPLYING THE CHANGE PROCESS

Working in teams, participants will apply a structured format to actual change situations within their operating environment in order to put into practice all of the elements of the program. Each team will prepare a proposal and strategy to measurably improve the desired outcomes of the change.

Facing the Challenges of Change

In this highly interactive task, the group must organize and work efficiently in teams to achieve a performance goal and quality standard for a new product. Innovative measures must be undertaken in order for the company to remain competitive in the marketplace. To be successful, the teams will need to overcome issues such as resistance to change, self-imposed barriers and unexpected changes from management. External competitive pressures and time-sensitive implementation schedules add an increased sense of urgency to the challenge.

The Impact of Change

In a boardroom format, participants will evaluate the results and the overall performance of the change simulation. Teams will collectively analyze the project to determine how to improve and strengthen the process of change.

Accountability for Behavior (optional re-assessment)

The participants will receive and evaluate progress toward their goals which were set in Round One (The Leadership Advantage Program). The leadership pattern results will provide a comparison of where they "were" and where they "are now" in relation to the perception of their leadership behavior by associates.

Managing the Dynamics of Change (Harvard Case Study)

In this real-life case study of a major US company, participants analyze the powerful influences and forces that may impact an organization in transition. The case study engages the group in a spirited dialogue on the various issues related to this company's experience with change and provides additional summary and perspective on the many topics discussed throughout the program.

Beyond the Boundaries

Transforming Culture

The ***Beyond the Boundaries Workshop*** is transforming your culture (team, department, division, or organization), and is an activity-based workshop centered on strengthening the effectiveness of your team's operating environment and the ongoing working relationships within that atmosphere. Prior to the program, the team members and selected associates will complete two instruments, the Leadership Effectiveness Profile (LEP) and the Organizational Culture Inventory (OCI). You and your team will explore various perceptions of the environment (shown in the LEP and OCI results) compared with expectations and identify and develop action plans for closing potential gaps and improving the team's efficiency and effectiveness.

During This Workshop, You and Your Team Will Work Together To:

- Identify the ideal culture for your team or operating environment

- Explore and evaluate OCI trends that are supporting or hindering your team's desired results

- Analyze and discuss a case study relevant to creating and sustaining a healthy, productive and successful culture

- Actively engage in a management simulation where participants experience the issues first-hand that help or hinder an effective culture, and

- Participate in team focus sessions and proactive planning activities designed to build a strategy for closing the gap between the current culture and the ideal environment identified by the team

Specific Outcomes

These Will Vary Based on the Priority Needs of Each Team, But in General the Team Will:

- Understand the current culture, its strengths and weaknesses, and the changes needed to meet present and future goals
- Strengthen the alignment of vision, mission, and goals
- Promote a sense of accountability to motivate members of the team to work towards establishing and achieving a more desired performance-driven culture with clear and measurable goals
- Enrich and strengthen communications to build and sustain valued partnerships between associates, peers, management, and customers
- Increase comfort to support innovation and creativity in the operating environment, and
- Identify the barriers and potential roadblocks to building a more effective operating environment

And as a Result:

- Develop more creative, innovative solutions to problems
- Develop more productive operating practices
- Create more effective communications
- Minimize workplace disruption from team conflict and misunderstood objectives
- Create more efficient and effective planning and implementation cycles
- Experience a higher percentage of successful plan execution, and
- Create specific action plans (including accountability, timelines, measurement methods) based on the work group's issues.

Intentional and Purposeful Leadership

Coaching and Consulting

The *Intentional & Purposeful Leadership Coaching & Consulting packages* include:

- a six-month concierge-type service process with assessments
- 8 - 10 coaching sessions
- re-assessment 6-12 months later to determine progress toward goals
- monthly tips/articles
- email access to a coach for six months
- conversations with participant's manager pre and post process
- a midpoint discussion for progress

Executive Leadership & Mid to Senior Level Management

We partner with successful leaders in determining key patterns of behavior that help or hinder them in achieving their greatest success. We work with leaders who are willing and motivated to change their behavior to improve their leadership performance and effectiveness.

Emerging Leaders & High-Performers

We assist new leaders in developing behaviors that will ensure greater success. We provide support in developing leadership traits that align the organization's goals with their own core values and beliefs. Participant receives feedback on the perception of their leadership style through a 360-degree feedback assessment. This feedback provides awareness and a starting point for discussion and setting target goals.

Team/Group: Series of 1/2 Day Sessions

We assist teams/groups/divisions/cross-functional teams in improving their collective effectiveness and performance. We explore counter-productive behaviors and assist the team in productivity. We explore positive ways to resolve conflicts, encouraging impassioned discussions while maintaining respect for all contributors. We ask that groups involve all key members of their team and all stakeholders in soliciting valuable feedback. We work with groups who are willing and motivated to change their behaviors to improve their team's performance and effectiveness.

Presentation and Communication Coaching

How you communicate impacts your ability to reach your full potential – from the words you use to the questions you ask. Presentation and Communication skills coaching is for:

- Leaders who are looking to take their skills to the next level
- Sales professionals looking to pitch their products and services more effectively
- Professionals who are looking to speak to a large audience or at a conference
- Individuals who want to "own the room" when it really counts

We will assess your needs and work with you (or your group) to achieve your communication goals.

About LeadAdvantage, Inc.

LeadAdvantage, Inc., a leadership and team development company, has consulted both in the US and internationally, to strengthen behavior and promote effective organizational change.

LeadAdvantage offers expertise in facilitating a business-relevant, engaging and high-energy leadership process. This process creates an environment where leaders are individually equipped to navigate successfully through your specific business challenges to achieve a desired objective.

LeadAdvantage combines experience gained from working with managers and executives around the world with a unique facilitation style that is unparalleled in the industry. Every facilitator has a corporate management background offering direct and relevant experience with leadership issues faced by individuals and organizations.

What we do:

- Leadership and Team Development, High-Potential Processes, Coaching and Consulting
- Partner with clients to advance corporate and/or team culture to achieve both top-line and bottom-line results
- Promote greater trust, effective collaboration and high-performance work teams, and individual employee development.

How we do it:

- Validated assessments
- Business simulations and case studies
- Awareness of self and peer influential patterns of behavior

Why it makes a difference:

- Unifies and improves decision-making
- Minimizes counter-productive actions
- Strengthens behaviors that enhance communication & performance

To contact us:

Sherri K. Baldwin
Principal, LeadAdvantage, Inc.
704-577-7891
LeadAdvantageInc.com

Client Comments About
LeadAdvantage's Leadership Process

Melissa - Duke Energy, Scientist:

"The material that Sherri and Rick presented was very well structured and presented often with humor or dynamic learning activities, but in a way that made you remember the concepts while having fun. Most importantly the training allowed me to have a rare good, bad, or ugly look at myself through others' eyes. Our coworkers completed anonymous surveys for each participant and the results were presented to us at the end of the session. Sherri and Rick had a one on one session to discuss the results privately with each participant. This was probably the most valuable piece of information from the program. Sherri coached me on what I needed to do to improve or change my perception among my peers and helped me figure out how to effectively communicate with my coworkers according to their personality and leadership traits that I can now identify on the spot."

Laura - Executive Director

"With a communications background, I have been through several types of leadership programs, but Rick and Sherri have proved they are two of the best in the business. The executive coaching, goals and insights they give each individual is unparalleled in my opinion. They truly care about your growth and want to see each participant succeed."

Brad – Manager, National Gypsum

"Most management courses provide programs that focus on motivating employees, how to delegate and use time efficiently. However, Leadership Advantage takes an outside of the box approach to building and motivating teams that centers on personality dynamics and interpersonal compatibilization. To do this, the LeadAdvantage team systematically defines many personality types and explores how these personality dynamics communicate and interact with each other depending on the situation and relationship (i.e. direct report, colleague, or boss).

In categorically defining these fundamental personality traits, a manager can recognize their own personality tendencies, and the personalities in their own team, to leverage each personality type to each task and make a team excel. I recommend this program to anyone who wants to truly understand the dynamics of their team."

www.ingramcontent.com/pod-product-compliance
Lightning Source LLC
Chambersburg PA
CBHW070405200326
41518CB00011B/2075